TOWARDS THE CREATIVE TEACHING OF ENGLISH

Editor: LOU SPAVENTA

Towards the Creative Teaching of English

MAGGIE MELVILLE
LYDIA LANGENHEIM
LOU SPAVENTA
MARIO RINVOLUCRI

Edited by LOU SPAVENTA

London
GEORGE ALLEN & UNWIN
Boston   Sydney

GEORGE ALLEN & UNWIN LTD
40 Museum Street, London WC1A 1LU

© George Allen & Unwin (Publishers) Ltd, 1980

British Library Cataloguing in Publication Data

Towards the creative teaching of English.
  1. English language—Study and teaching—Foreign students
  I. Melville, Maggie   II. Spaventa, Lou
  428′.2′407   PE1128.A2   80-40405

ISBN 0-04-371074-3

Set in 10 on 12 point Times by Trade Linotype Ltd., Birmingham
and printed in Great Britain
by Biddles Ltd., Guildford, Surrey

Acknowledgement

This book is a coming together of four slimmer volumes as mentioned above. As little editing as possible has been done in order to preserve the individual voice of each writer. Editing was largely confined to questions of overall style and questions of text clarity.

Since some individuals who worked on the initial versions of each section as separate texts did not work on the compilation of the four texts, I would like to acknowledge typists, proof readers and guiding spirits, whose earlier work paved the way for the present book. They are: John Gray, Michael Langenheim, Julie Fettes, Mario Rinvolucri, Saxon Menne, Janice Abbot and Bernard Dufeu specifically for Tasks 10, 17 and 16 of 'Teacherless Tasks', and Sue Ford. In addition, thanks to the following language schools where materials were tested: the New School, Davies', and the Cambridge Academy of English. Thanks too to teachers and students with whom we have worked over the years.

I would also like to thank the following publishers for allowing us to reproduce material: Eyre Methuen Ltd for Old Times (Act one) by Harold Pinter; Charles Scribner's Sons for *The Great Gatsby* by F. Scott Fitzgerald; Universities Federation for Animal Welfare. *The Centipede* by Mrs Edmund Craster.

LOU SPAVENTA
CANTERBURY
NOVEMBER 1979

The authors of this book are an experienced team of Teachers and Teacher Trainers. They have all taught on numerous training courses for ELT teachers run by Pilgrims English Language Courses and held at the University of Kent in Canterbury.

If you would like some information about these courses, please write to:

Course Enquiries (GAU)
Pilgrims Language Courses Ltd
8 Vernon Place
Canterbury
Kent CT1 3YG
England

Telephone Nos: (0227) 69127/63052
Telex No: 695633

Contents

Preface

This book has grown out of good ideas that were encouraged and given space and time to mature. Since the middle of the seventies, Pilgrims Language Courses of Canterbury, has held intensive summer EFL courses at the University of Kent. The concept underlying Pilgrims' success in these courses has been that of giving pedagogical freedom to a small group of creative teachers. These teachers have shaped the nature of things at Pilgrims Language Courses and in turn have been shaped by the forces of their own momentum.

The present volume of teaching techniques and ideas is a compilation of the work of four of those teachers. Originally, each section in this book was a small book standing alone, used time and again by teachers who were looking for things to do in the EFL class or for ideas to start them thinking about what they could do in the EFL class. Each author of each section was once told, 'That's a good idea. I liked your session today. Have you ever thought of putting this all down in a book so that others could use your ideas?' The result of such encouragements has been a series of slim volumes on many aspects of EFL. The four volumes that comprise the four sections of this book were once part of that series. The present four were chosen because they represent at least three of the tenets which some Pilgrims teachers, and of course, many others, share. These are:

> language learning is whole person learning
> the content of the language lesson should be the student
> the teacher should learn to withdraw creatively to give learning space to the students.

None of these concepts is radically new. They have all been talked about for quite some time. What is new is the application of these concepts. In the exercises in this book, directions are explicitly given with these three teaching tenets in mind. The guiding and unifying principle of the book emerges through the application of the three tenets. This principle, briefly stated, is that in order for real learning to take place, there must be a degree of trust and honesty in the relationship of student to teacher and student to student. Real learning comes about when the learner is in a receptive state, not when he is defending himself from the onslaughts of the foreign language through teacher, text or tape. The approach might be called a broad humanistic one, with no particular philosophy or philosopher behind it; just the general acknowledgement that the classroom situation is, after all, a dialogue between people, and that people is the subject matter of the language course.

Language Learning is Whole Person Learning

This aphorism comes from the work of Charles Curran, who through a counseling approach to the learning situation, has shown many of us that the proper subject of study in the language classroom is the person and his relation to others in the class group. This is to say that the teacher profits by whatever insight he can gain into the very human processes of group-formation and realisation of self in the group. The work of Curran is not the subject here, but the willing reader is advised to seek out any of the following titles:

Counseling-Learning in Second Languages—1976
Counseling-Learning A Whole-Person Model for Education—1977
Counseling and Psychotherapy: The Pursuit of Values—1976

All by Charles A. Curran and available through Apple River Press, Apple River, Illinois, 61001, USA.

On another level, the idea of learning with the whole person relates to the infamous idea of talking heads. Talking heads were once the norm of the language classroom. They were disembodied talkers of a foreign language, empty of movement and expression. The exercises using drama techniques in the first two sections of this book attempt to get the human juices flowing, to get people moving about and expressing themselves. Many language classes are predictably boring because everyone knows where he'll be and what he'll do during that hour; for example, sitting in the first row first seat near the window watching the cars out in the street while Mrs Toast drills the class on être. 'English through Drama' and 'Am I Me?' try to get the student involved and actively using the language, with all that entails of gesture, expression, body language and voice control. 'Teacherless Tasks' involves the student to an extent whereby he cannot and does not want to withdraw from the group, and whereby the contribution of the weakest student can weigh as heavily as that of the strongest one.

The Content of the Language Lesson Should Be the Student

This might be phrased another way to focus more directly on the task of the teacher, and that is, 'The job of the teacher is to work on the student, while the student works on the language.' The teacher is often seen as a disseminator of the truth, ie, the foreign language, and as the final arbiter of right and wrong. The focus in most language classrooms has been frontal, toward the teacher. Group work is often time-serving because the final step is a return to the word of the teacher, thereby nullifying the truth of what went on in the group. When the teacher allows the concerns and cares of the students to shape the direction of the class, then he is following the dictum that the content of the language lesson should be the student.

The content of the language lesson can be what the student knows, what he wants to know, and what he cares about, what he wants to talk about. To be more concrete, let us say that at one end of the spectrum is the prepared language lesson which goes according to a fixed syllabus and does not deviate, and at the other end of this content spectrum is the lesson in which the students determine entirely the content of the lesson, a good example here would be a Community Language Learning class (*cf* Curran, *Counseling-Learning in Second Languages*). The exercises in 'Music, Music, Music,' try to take into account the real strength of interest engendered by a student-centred content to the language lesson. When a student talks about what he saw or did or felt, he talks with authority and with interest.

One might ask, 'If the student finds himself infinitely exciting to talk about, how will anyone else get a chance to speak?' This concern or others like it might be legitimate if the student were talking to a herd of cattle. However, the idea of one person monopolising class time becomes less compelling when the other people in the class are taken into account, because the other people will react to one student's theft of time. They will let him know, either directly or indirectly. One of the reasons that student-determined class content is effective is that in the very act of giving students the right to make decisions about what goes on in the class, the teacher has acknowledged a human relationship, a sharing situation, a step in the demystification of the teacher's role.

The Teacher Should Learn to Withdraw Creatively to Give More Space to the Students

This last maxim relates in part to the discussion on student-centred lessons, for when the student has contributed to the content of learning he will also contribute to the way it is learned. The teacher must learn to give the student space in which to move, both physically and mentally. This means that all the classroom is open to all the people in it—no no man's land between the teacher's desk and those of the students. This also means that psychologically the teacher must not crowd the student. He must leave him room to think, to mull over what has been said, to make decisions about the language under study. Furthermore, the teacher must recognise that in a class of thirty students, there may be thirty different needs for space. Lock-step practice is no practice at all. Each student learns at his own pace. The job of the teacher is to facilitate that learning by offering intelligent choices, by feeding the student more information when he is ready and not before, and by making the circumstances of learning positive. 'Teacherless Tasks' has an introductory section which will lead the interested teacher in this direction without too much need to fear failure or anxiety because of novelty.

The exercises in this book are ideas for

classwork and points of departure for further development on the part of teacher and students. They are imperfect and unfinished because they lack the final touch that only comes with actualisation. As they stand in this book, they are as mounted butterflies. The teacher and students in the classroom can give them the breath of life again. Teaching and learning is a process and because of this it is only realised in the doing. These activities that follow are products of the process of teaching and learning. There is always room for improvement and improvisation. All who use this book are welcome to write to the authors through the publisher or to Pilgrims Language Courses, 8 Vernon Place, Canterbury, Kent CT1 3YG.

LOU SPAVENTA
Canterbury, November 1979

1 *English Through Drama*

MAGGIE MELVILLE

1.1 INTRODUCTION

1.1.1 WHAT IS 'ENGLISH THROUGH DRAMA'?
It is a selection of supplementary material based on roleplay and imagination games. The aim is to stimulate natural spontaneous spoken English, and to help the student use language that is both grammatically correct and appropriate as defined by place or mood.

1.1.2 WHO IS IT FOR?
The lessons cover a range of ability from lower intermediate to advanced levels. They are suitable both for students who have a good knowledge of the English language and for students meeting English for the first time. In both cases, these lessons offer the opportunity to revise and reinforce orally structures that have already been acquired and, at the same time, provide a new learning environment.

1.1.3 WHY USE IT?
The lessons are student-centred, leaving the teacher free to give individual attention to students who need help and correction. The lessons are quick to prepare. The lessons are fun to do.

1.1.4 HOW DO YOU USE IT?
The age-group, level, number of students per group, time of the lesson, and specific aim are indicated at the beginning of each section or lesson. A brief set of instructions follows, plus, if applicable, possible variations on the theme.

Age-group: The ages given are only a guide, not strictly chosen bounds.

Level: The level indicated is a guide for the teacher. The approach is the same for any level indicated, although the execution of the exercise and the time might well vary according to the class.

Number of Students: The number indicated is intended as a guide for the teacher.

Time: The time it takes to complete each activity depends on the level of the students. A good rule is to draw the lesson to a close while the students are still enjoying themselves, so that they will enjoy themselves a second and a third time.

Aim: Each lesson is centred on a particular area of language within the general aim of stimulating oral work.

1.2 ARRANGING THE CLASSROOM

As these lessons involve group work and presentation of individual group work to the class as a whole, it is helpful to arrange the seats in a semicircular or horseshoe shape if possible. Thus the teacher can be a member of the group or apart from it. There is an audience area and a sketch or mime area.

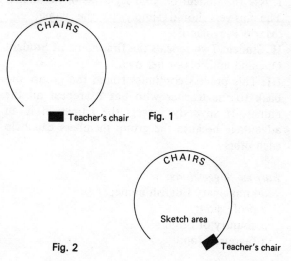

CHAIRS

■ Teacher's chair   Fig. 1

CHAIRS

Sketch area

■ Teacher's chair

Fig. 2

1.2.1 GROUPING

The following grouping technique enables the teacher to divide the class quickly and efficiently and to split up natural groups. For example:

1. If there are twenty students in the class, and five groups of four are required, the teacher gives each student a number from the sequence 1, 2, 3, 4; repeating the sequence five times. There will, therefore, be four students with 1, four with 2, four with 3, and four with 4. Students who have the same number form a group.

2. For pair work, designate one student A and one student B in each pair. The A student in each group has one set of instructions and the B student another.

3. Draw a sheet of symbols—six bowler hats, six pipes, six saucepans, etc. Cut the symbols out and put them into a pack. Each student takes a card and forms a group with the other students who have drawn the same symbol.

In the same way, students can be divided by being given sets of words, all those with the same word forming a group.

1.3   A WAY OF STARTING A LESSON

Age-group: all ages
Level: lower intermediate to advanced
Group size: five to twenty students
Time: ten to fifteen minutes
Aim: to concentrate the attention of the group on a particular subject; to unite the group
I. Ask the student on your right his or her name. The answer should simply be the name, e.g. 'Mario Rinvolucri'.
II. Student Two repeats the first name of Student One and adds his or her own.
III. This process continues round the group and back to the teacher who has to repeat all the names. If anybody forgets the names, it is an advantage because the group members can help each other.

Further Suggestions:
    an imaginary English name;
    a profession;
    a country of origin;
    a favourite food.

1.4   TENSE DRILLS THROUGH MIME

Age group: all ages
Level: lower intermediate to upper intermediate
Group size: five to twenty students
Time: half an hour
Aim: to practise tenses
Prepare a short mime and present it to the students. Ask the students questions about the mime using the tense that is to be practised.
I. Choose a title which determines the tense.
II. Prepare a mime which includes about five actions. Your choice depends on the students' knowledge of vocabulary, and on whether you want them to revise or to learn.

Examples:
    'What do I do every morning?'
    'What am I doing at the moment?'
    'What did I do last night?'
    'What do I sometimes/always/usually do?'
    'What will I never do?'
    'What will I do if I win a lot of money?'
    'What would you do if your car broke down?'
    'What have I just done?'
    'What would you have done if you had lived in the middle ages?'

III. Write the title on the blackboard. Present the mime twice simply and clearly. Exaggerate the movements.

1.4.1 EVERY MORNING (Lower intermediate to intermediate level)

The five actions are:
    1. waking up at eight o'clock;
    2. having a shower;
    3. getting dressed;
    4. having a cup of tea;
    5. reading the newspaper.
The mime is acted in the following stages:
1. You are asleep in bed. You wake up. You look at the clock. You show that it's eight o'clock with your fingers.
2. You stand under a shower, turn on the water, and after a while, turn it off.
3. You open a cupboard, take out some clothes and put them on.
4. You sit down, pick up a cup and drink from it.

5. You pick up a newspaper, open it and read it.
You then ask the class questions.

Teacher: 'What do I do every morning?'

Student One: 'You are sleeping.'

You as the teacher look puzzled, mime waking up again, and repeat the question.

Student Two: 'You woke up.'

You shake your head.

Student Three: 'You wake up.'

You nod your head and hold up eight fingers.

Student Three: 'You wake up at eight o'clock.'

Continue the questioning until all the students have repeated all the actions.

1.4.2 LAST NIGHT (Lower intermediate to intermediate)

The five actions are:

1. the telephone ringing;
2. answering the telephone;
3. taking a taxi;
4. going to the theatre;
5. having dinner.

The mime is acted in the following stages:

1. Make telephone noises.
2. Pick up the receiver. Listen and nod your head.
3. Stand in taxi-hailing position. Open the taxi door and get in.
4. Sit facing the students. Look as if you are enjoying something. Applaud.
5. Sit at table. Look at a menu. Eat and drink.

Then ask the class:

Teacher: 'What happened last night?'

Student One: 'The telephone rang.'

You the teacher look pleased at this response and motion for the other students to repeat what Student One has said.

Student Two: The telephone rang and you picked it up.'

You shake your head.

Student Three: 'The telephone rang and you answered it.'

1.4.3 WHAT WOULD YOU DO IF YOUR CAR BROKE DOWN? (Upper intermediate)

The five actions are:

1. trying to start the car;
2. opening the bonnet;
3. looking in the manual;

4. trying to start the car again;
5. hitching a lift.

The mime is acted in the following stages:

1. Look miserable. Switch on the ignition. Look puzzled.
2. Get out of the car. Open the bonnet. Look around inside. Look enlightened.
3. Get into the car. Look in the manual. Look triumphant.
4. Switch on the ignition. Look very miserable or cross.
5. Get out of the car. Lock the door. Stand in hitch-hiking position.

You then ask:

Teacher: 'What would I do if my car broke down?'

Student One: 'You would try to start the car again.'

You then look not quite satisfied.

Student Two: 'You'd try to start the car again.'

You look pleased.

1.4.4 WHAT HAVE I JUST DONE? (Intermediate)

The five actions are:

1. writing a letter;
2. putting the letter into an envelope;
3. finding the address;
4. sticking the stamp on;
5. posting the letter.

The mime is acted in the following stages:

1. Start writing the letter. Sit thinking. Finish the letter.
2. Fold the paper in three. Put it into an envelope. Seal the envelope.
3. Pick up the book. Look for the address. Write the address on the envelope.
4. Pick up the stamp. Lick it and stick it on the envelope.
5. Pick up the letter. Walk to a different part of the room. Post the letter and walk away.

Proceed with questions as in previous mimes. Repeat actions and stop after each stage to ask questions.

IV: Have a student prepare a mime and another student answer the questions. Repeat the process as often as necessary. Vary the questions:

'What does he/she do every day?'

'*What do we/they always do?*' (In this case, two or more students would present the mime.)

Watch out for over-complicated mimes. Try to keep the actions in the mime down to a minimum.

1.5 QUESTIONS THROUGH MIME

Age group: all ages
Level: lower intermediate to upper intermediate
Group size: five to twenty students
Time: half an hour
Aim: to practise questions and, in particular, to practise the conditional with contracted forms
I. write down mimes on pieces of paper and give one to each pair of students.

For example:
1. You are playing cards and one of you is cheating.
2. Someone gives you a birthday present and you don't like it.
3. You have invited someone to dinner but have forgotten all about it.
   The guest arrives. You are having dinner in front of the television.
4. (A mime for three students). You are waiting at the bus stop. You see someone stealing someone else's wallet.
5. You are in a hotel. You go to have a bath. You run the water, get in, and start washing. Unbeknown to you, there is someone in the shower. The person reaches out to get a towel.
II. Write the following on the blackboard:
   'What would you do if...?'
   'I'd...'
III. When the students are ready, explain what happens next:
1. Have one student leave the room.
2. A pair of students show their mime to the rest of the class. (It should be discussed briefly to make sure that everybody has got it right.)
3. Have the student who went out of the room return. Ask him to try to guess what the mime was about by asking everybody in the group this question:
   'What would you do if this happened to you?'
   The other students respond with: 'I'd...'

When everybody has answered, different questions can be asked.

For example:
   'Are you in a...?'
   'Is it about a...?', and so on.
   The same process is repeated until all the mimes have been seen.

1.6 PREPOSITIONS AND PHRASAL VERBS THROUGH MIME

Age group: all ages
Level: lower intermediate to advanced
Group size: five to twenty students
Time: half an hour
Aim: to practise prepositions and phrasal verbs
I. Choose as a subject for your mime something which involves detail. Prepare carefully so that each detail is clear. Present the mime to the students. They tell you in detail what you are doing.
   Here are some suggestions:
   boiling an egg;
   doing up a shoelace;
   reading a newspaper;
   lighting a match;
   putting on lipstick;
   peeling a banana.
   Here is an example: taking a coat out of a cupboard.
1. Open the cupboard door.
2. Reach into the cupboard.
3. Take out the coat.
4. Take the coat off the hanger.
5. Put the hanger on the rail.
6. Put on the coat.
II. Each student prepares a mime to present to the class.
A. Each student chooses a subject, and at home actually tries out the chosen subject, writing down each step as a set of instructions.
B. The instructions are read out one by one to another student who acts them out without knowing what the subject is. If the instructions are correct the mime will be clear.

What to watch out for: tenses that should be used.

The past ____le is the most natural, but the present s____ and continuous can be used. The teacher ____ choose the tense by asking the appropr____ uestion.

'How ____ ou boil an egg?'
'Wh____ I do?'
'Wh____ I doing?'

1.6.1 BOILING AN EGG

1. Pick up a pan.
2. Go to the sink.
3. Turn on the tap.
4. Fill the pan with water.
5. Turn off the tap.
6. Put the pan on a hot plate.
7. Switch on.
8. Open the fridge door.
9. Take out an egg.
10. Put the egg in the pan.
11. Sit down.
12. Look at your watch.
13. Get up.
14. Open a drawer.
15. Take out a spoon.
16. Take the egg out of the pan with the spoon.
17. Put the egg in an eggcup.

1.6.2 DOING UP A SHOELACE

1. Sit down.
2. Bend over.
3. Bring your hands down to your shoe.
4. Cross left shoelace over right shoelace.
5. Bring the end of the left shoelace under the right one.
6. Pull left and right shoelace.
7. Make a loop with the left shoelace.
8. Cross right shoelace over left one.
9. Make a loop with the right shoelace.
10. Bring right loop under left one.
11. Pull both loops.

1.6.3 READING A NEWSPAPER

1. Pick up a newspaper.
2. Look at the front page.
3. Lay the paper down.
4. Hold sides of the paper.
5. Bring left hand to right hand.
6. Move left hand in an arc to a position double the original distance between the two hands.
7. Repeat steps five and six.
8. Read the paper.

1.6.4 LIGHTING A MATCH

1. Pick up a match box.
2. Push out the tray with your thumb.
3. Take out a match.
4. Bring the match to the side of the box.
5. Strike the match towards you or away from you.

1.6.5 PUTTING ON LIPSTICK

1. Pick up a lipstick.
2. Pull off the cap.
3. Swivel the base.
4. Open your mouth.
5. Look into a mirror.
6. Put on the lipstick.

1.6.6 PEELING A BANANA

1. Hold a banana in your right hand.
2. Break off the top of the banana with your left hand.
3. Peel the top down to the base making an arc the size of the banana.

1.7 VOCABULARY THROUGH MIME

Age group: teenagers and adults
Level: lower intermediate to advanced
Group size: five to twenty students
Time: twenty minutes
Aim: to increase vocabulary through one-action mimes performed by the teacher and students in turn, using a chair as a stimulus
Materials: a chair

I. The teacher, and then each student in turn, shows through mime a real use for a chair or a place where a chair is used or where the idea of sitting is given.

The other students guess what the chair is, where it is or what it is being used for.

For example:
a car seat;

something to stand upon to change a light bulb;
something to put your feet up on;
something to put against a door to keep it shut or open;
  in a cinema;
  at a desk;
  at the dentist's;
  a bicycle;
  a horse;
something to defend yourself with.

II. The teacher, and each student in turn, shows a mime using a chair as anything imaginable which is suggested by its shape.

The other students guess what the chair is.

For example:
  a pram;
  a lawnmower;
  someone to dance with;
  a telephone;
  a machine gun;
  a spade;
  a hoover;
  a table;
  a typewriter;
  a hat;
  a brush;
  a shield.

What to watch out for: the teacher must be ready with new vocabulary and perhaps write it on the board to revise later on.

A suggestion: Do this exercise with a large sheet of paper; a soft woolly hat; an imaginary stick shape; an imaginary round shape.

1.8 WAYS OF STIMULATING ORAL NARRATIVE WORK

Age group: all ages
Level: intermediate to advanced
Group size: five to twenty students
Time: about half an hour for each technique
Aim: oral practice

1.8.1 STORY TELLING FROM IMAGINATION GAMES AND WORD ASSOCIATION

I. One student says a word. Then the next student says a word that he associates with the first word. The next student says a word that he associates with the second word, and so on until each student has said a word.

For example:
  knife;   death;
  wound;   murder;
  pain;   police;
  agony;   prison.

The teacher and/or a student tell a story using all the words.

For example

The knife cut deep. He put his hand to the wound. The pain was terrible, and he fell in agony to the floor. Death soon followed. This was murder. The police were in no doubt. A prison was the scene of the crime.

II. *VARIATIONS*

1. Every word must begin with the same letter.
2. Every word must start with the final letter of the previous word.
3. Every word must start with the final sound of the previous word. This is useful for pronunciation as the final sound is often very different from the final letter, e.g. *church* to *cheese* instead of *church* to *house*.
4. Take a sentence like, 'The Smiths' cat is a . . . cat.' Each student adds an adjective from A-Z describing the cat. Each student repeats what the others have said before adding his adjective.

What to watch out for: As the words come from the students, they should be able to use them in telling a story, whichever level they are. Be ready to add new vocabulary where necessary.

1.8.2 SENTENCE CHAIN

Possible Aims: Tense drills and use of adjectives and adverbs.

I. *TENSE DRILLS* The teacher begins a story and each student adds a sentence.

For example:

'Sammy Smith's Habits' (to practise the present simple and time adverbs)

Sammy Smith always smokes a pipe but he never smokes cigarettes. He sits in front of the television with his feet up, and he sometimes falls asleep . . .

'In the Middle of the Night' (to practise past continuous and simple past)

I was lying in bed when I heard the door creak. I thought I was dreaming. Then I saw a light . . .

II. *ADJECTIVES* The teacher begins a story. Each student adds a sentence that contains a superlative.

For example:

'The Browns' Cat' (to practise the superlative of adjectives)

The Browns' cat is the most aggressive cat. The Browns' cat is the most beautiful cat . . .

III. *ADVERBS* The teacher begins a story. Each student adds a sentence that contains an adverb.

For example:

'All about Mr Smith'

Mr Smith looks admiringly at pretty girls. He plays the piano beautifully, and he drives carefully . . .

IV. *SUGGESTIONS* Each student repeats what the other students have said before adding his or her own sentence. In a group of twenty try to avoid excessive story-length. Split a group of twenty into two groups of ten students each. The last student in each group finishes the story.

1.8.3 CHAIN STORY

The teacher begins a story. The students finish it individually or in groups. The group or the individual prepares the ending in writing. The students listen to each other's versions, and finally listen to the actual ending of the story.

I. *SAMPLE STORIES* A. Last year a man was driving along the road in the late evening. He saw a hitchhiker at the side of the road—a girl. He stopped the car and asked her where she wanted to go. As it happened she was going home and as she lived very near his home, he told her to get in and he said that he would take her straight to her door as he had to go in that direction. At first she insisted that it wasn't necessary, but he insisted and finally she agreed.

By this time they had arrived. She got out of the car, said goodbye, went up the steps, and in through the front door. He didn't even have time to ask her name, which was a shame; however, he decided to forget about it.

A few weeks later he was driving past the same way and was tempted to call in and see if she was there, as try as he might, he couldn't forget her. He stopped the car outside the house and thinking that it was now or never decided to go and knock at the door. The door opened, but instead of it being the girl he expected, he saw a woman of about forty. He thought that he had perhaps made a mistake, but although he didn't know her name he tried to describe the girl to the woman and he asked if she lived next door. The woman looked at him very carefully and without saying whether she knew the girl or not, asked him questions about why he was looking for her, and where he had met her. He told her, and he felt that he needed to explain all that he knew. She took a deep breath and asked him to come in and sit down as she had something to tell him . . .

The End of the Story The woman was the girl's mother and she was used to people coming to ask for her daughter as she had often hitchhiked home and had met a lot of people that way. The only difference this time being that two years ago her daughter had been in a serious accident which had occurred at the very place where the man had picked her up. She was dead but she still tried to come home.

B. The moon was just coming up, and its pale light shone over the bay. Everything was silent, except for the sound of the waves gently breaking on the beach. Across the bay the lights of the various houses were beginning to twinkle.

A man emerged from the shadows and began to walk across the beach towards the sea. Halfway across the beach he stopped, and looked out over the sea. He seemed to be waiting.

Time went by, then directly opposite him, on the other side of the bay, a light went on. He lifted one arm eagerly towards the light as if to touch it, and stood gazing across the calm water. Then he turned, walked slowly back, and disappeared once more into the shadows.

What magic did that light hold for him? What secret force drew him from the shadows, to gaze longingly at a light in the darkness? The answer lay... (from *The Great Gatsby* by F. Scott Fitzgerald)

The End of the Story... in the light that came from Daisy's house, the woman Gatsby loved.

C. The Taylors had recently moved into a new house. It had always been their dream to have a house of their own and now it had come true. Life was very busy while they were moving in, the children were still on holiday and Mrs Taylor had her hands full. But now term had started and everything was almost back to normal.

It was a terraced house, with a little garden at the back and at the front. The upstairs windows had a small balcony, which gave the house its charm. The back door led from the garden into the kitchen, and it was in this room that Mrs Taylor was sitting sewing, on the first peaceful day she had had for weeks.

She was waiting for her son to come home from school; the others would be home later as they were at a different school and had further to come. She heard him come running up to the back door. The door opened and she called out 'Hello,' but he didn't answer. She got up, and she went and looked outside but she couldn't see him. Then she heard footsteps on the stairs; whoever it was ran across the landing and into the main bedroom. She thought that her son was trying to frighten her, and had somehow managed to get past without her seeing because her head was bent over her sewing. So she went upstairs and called out again, but there was no answer. She looked in all the rooms, but there was no one there.

Finally she went back down to the kitchen. She heard the footsteps again; the door opened but this time there was her son. 'What have you been

doing?' she asked. 'Why did you go running upstairs like that?' He looked surprised, 'I've just got back, what do you mean?' Then she remembered a story they had been told just before they bought the house. About...

The End of the Story... a hundred years ago, a little boy heard his parents arriving. He came in through the back door and ran up the stairs into his parents' bedroom, and out onto the balcony to welcome them. The wooden rail was rotten, he leant on it and fell to his death.

D. The doctor was a man dedicated to science and above all to sharing his knowledge with those under his guidance. He led a simple life divided between his family and his work at the hospital. He was well liked by his students who respected his sincere approach to his work and his desire to be given the chance to help mankind to the best of his ability.

At this moment he was alone in the laboratory, working quietly and carefully on an experiment for the afternoon's lesson. Suddenly there was an earth-shattering crash. Everything went dark and the sound of wind roaring filled his ears. He was thrown to the ground. Thoughts flashed through his mind, of his wife, of the students, of the doctors and nurses, and of the sick people in the hospital. What was happening? Was it the end of the world?

The End of the Story The doctor in a hospital in Nagasaki witnessed the atomic bomb and survived it. He lived for five years studying the effects of radioactivity on his own body.

II. *VARIATIONS* For language laboratory practice tape the beginning of the story. Have each student add his or her own ending. Then have the students change places and listen to each other's versions. Finally, have them listen to the actual version.

1.8.4 STORY FROM WORDS
I. Each student writes down any five words.
II. Two students put their words together making ten, and invent a dialogue using the ten words.

III. Each pair exchange their words with another pair, and think of another ten words. With the new list of twenty words, the pair invent a story or dialogue.

IV. *VARIATION* In the language laboratory, have each student think of a word. The words are reported to the group. The teacher records the beginning of a story using his word. Each student follows on from the teacher's beginning. The students then change booths and follow on, incorporating their words into the stories they find. Allow about four minutes for recording and then switch booths to completion.

1.8.5 STORY TELLING THROUGH MIME

I. Invent a story which can be divided into definite stages.

II. Teach the students signs for the set of instructions you need to use, eg 'Yes,' 'No,' 'Repeat,' and 'Tell the story from the beginning.'

III. Give the students new vocabulary if necessary.

IV. Begin the mime, stopping after each mimed action, to allow the students to tell the story.

V. Make sure that all the students repeat, and tell the story from the beginning.

VI. Have the students write the story.

Examples of Mime Stories

1. *Last Night:*
   (a) I was asleep.
   (b) I woke up.
   (c) I got out of bed.
   (d) I went downstairs.
   (e) I opened the front door.
   (f) I saw a baby on the doorstep.
   (g) it was crying.
   (h) I wondered what I could do.
   (i) I had an idea.
   (j) I picked the baby up.
   (k) I went next door.
   (l) I put the baby down outside the front door.

2. *This morning:*
   (a) I was reading.
   (b) I heard a knock at the front door.
   (c) I got up.
   (d) I went to the door.
   (e) I opened it.
   (f) There was no one there.
   (g) I looked down.
   (h) I saw a bunch of flowers.
   (i) I picked them up.
   (j) I was very pleased.
   (k) I read the card.
   (l) I was very disappointed.
   (m) I went next door.
   (n) I knocked at the door.
   (o) I put the flowers down.

3. *When I went shopping:*
   (a) I was looking at some earrings/pipes.
   (b) I saw a woman/man.
   (c) She/he had a big bag.
   (d) She/he picked up a watch.
   (e) And put it in her/his bag.
   (f) She/he picked up a lighter.
   (g) And put it in her/his bag.
   (h) The salesgirl saw everything.
   (i) She made a telephone call.
   (j) The woman/man went out of the shop.
   (k) A store detective was waiting outside.
   (l) He asked the woman/man to open her/his bag.
   (m) He found the watch and the lighter.
   (n) He also found a pair of earrings, a necklace, etc . . .

For this mime story you can differentiate the characters by wearing a hat for the woman/man, sunglasses for the store detective and so on.

4. *A tourist lost in London:*
   (a) I was lost.
   (b) I opened my bag.
   (c) I took out a map.
   (d) I looked for the road.
   (e) I couldn't find it.
   (f) I asked a policeman.
   (g) I listened very carefully.
   (h) I crossed the road.
   (i) I walked to the end of the road.
   (j) I turned left.
   (k) I turned right at the traffic lights.
   (l) I stopped and looked at the name of the road.
   (m) I was still lost.

5. *The launderette:* *watch in washing machine*

(a) I went to the launderette.
(b) I put my clothes in the machine.
(c) I poured the soap into the hole.
(d) I put my money in the slot.
(e) I sat down and waited.
(f) I looked at my watch.
(g) It wasn't there.
(h) I tried to remember where I had put it.
(i) I looked in my pocket.
(j) I looked in my bag.
(k) Then I remembered.
(l) I looked in the machine.
(m) I saw my watch.

1.9 QUESTIONS AND ROLEPLAY

1.9.1 ADJECTIVES: TEAPOTS

Age group: all ages
Level: lower intermediate to advanced
Group size: five to twenty students
Time: about half an hour depending on the size of the group
Aim: to learn the differences between adjectives used to describe objects and adjectives used to describe people

I. Draw a picture of a teapot on the blackboard. Describe a teapot which represents a famous person. Have the students guess who that person is by asking questions.
For example:

My teapot is big and brown. It comes from Africa. It has gold designs on it. It was often seen on television and in the newspapers.
Answer: Idi Amin

My teapot is made out of fine china. It is high and narrow. The lid is black and there are large green oval designs round the top. A lot of people drink this tea and enjoy it. It comes from Italy.
Answer: Sophia Loren

II. Have each student prepare a description of a teapot which represents a famous person. Get them to answer these questions:

Is your teapot old or new?
What size is/was your teapot? (big, small, medium)
What shape is/was your teapot? (round, square, narrow, wide)
What is/was it made of? (china, silver, pottery, some other material)
What colour is/was it?
Where is/was it?

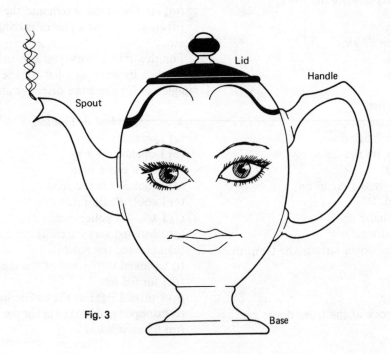

Fig. 3

Where does/did it come from?
What is/was the tea like?
When do/did people drink it?
Who drinks/drank it?

Think of other ways of describing the teapot. What are some other words to describe it?

Each student then describes his or her teapot to the class.

III. *VARIATIONS*

A. Each student prepares a description of a teapot, and the other students ask questions in order to find out who the person is.

B. Each student takes the role of a famous person. The other students ask questions in order to find out who the person is.

What to watch out for: The correct use of language for an object and for a person.

1.9.2 ADJECTIVES: OBJECTS

Age group: all ages
Level: lower intermediate to advanced
Group size: five to twenty students
Time: about an hour depending on the size of the group
Aim: to show the differences between adjectives used to describe objects and adjectives used to describe people
Materials: about ten different objects (a match box, a teaspoon, a stone, a comb, a plate, a dry leaf, a watch, an empty Coca-Cola tin, a glass, a glove).

I. Ask a student to close his eyes. Give the student an object and ask him to guess what it is and to describe it as far as possible. Revise or learn vocabulary through questions:

A. Is it hot or cold?
Is it rough or smooth?
Is it big or small?
Is it heavy or light?

Have the students think of other pairs of words which describe objects in this way.

B. What is it?
What is it made of?
Where does it come from?
Does it make a noise?

Can you open it?
Can you break it?

Have the students think of other questions which when answered would give words to describe the object.

Repeat the process with each student and each new object.

II. Ask each student to choose an object, and to choose four adjectives which best describe it.

For example:

A plate is smooth, cold, round, and two-sided. A dead leaf is dry, light, brittle, and fine.

A. Ask the students if they can use the adjectives which describe the object to describe people.

B. Have the students make a list of adjectives usable for both people and objects.

C. Ask each student to imagine a person to whom the four adjectives for the chosen object could also apply, and to describe this person to the group. The group guesses the object.

For example:

A very large person, perhaps someone who eats a lot. A person with a very carefully groomed exterior, who is unemotional and calculating and something of a hypocrite.

The object is the plate.

A small delicate person, very sensitive and perhaps very lonely.

The object is the dead leaf.

III. The students work in small groups, each choosing an object and following the previous part of the exercise. They build a character each. Each character is integrated into a sketch prepared by the group. On presentation of the sketch, the other class members write down the adjectives which describe the characters in the sketch, and then try to guess the original objects.

For example:

The plate is a psychoanalist, the leaf his patient. The patient tries to explain that he has a problem—loneliness. The psychoanalist doesn't really listen but is very polite.

IV. *SUGGESTIONS*

A. A character description.
B. Tape the sketches for playback.
C. Write down the dialogue.

1.9.3 QUESTION STRUCTURES

Age group: all ages
Level: lower intermediate to advanced
Group size: five to twenty students
Time: about an hour depending on the size of the group
Aim: to practise question structures
Materials: an assortment of hats
I. Show the students the hats.
A. Ask each student to choose a hat, but explain that at this stage they must not take the hat they have chosen because several people might have chosen the same one.
B. Ask the students to ask themselves the following questions about the hats they have chosen:
1. What's the name of the hat you have chosen?
2. What's it made of?
3. Who wears it?
4. When does he or she wear it?
5. What's his or her name?
6. Where does this person live?
7. Does this person work hard?
8. Does he or she earn a lot of money?
9. Does he or she have any children?
10. How old is this person?
11. Why does he or she wear a hat?
C. Ask each student to think of other ways to describe the owner of the hat.
D. Choose a hat and have the students who have chosen it give their descriptions. When several people have chosen the same hat, often very different ideas about who the hat belongs to arise in the process.
II. Ask one of the students to choose a hat, either the same one as before or a different one. Give him or her the hat, take the student outside the room and give him or her these instructions:
1. You are now going to take on the role of the owner of this hat.
2. You have come here today to talk to the group and to answer their questions.
3. Decide what your new name and your job is.
III. Prepare the class for a visitor in the following way:
'Today . . . School/College has great pleasure in presenting someone who has led a life of great interest to you. They have most kindly agreed to come here today and answer the many questions you will have.'

Go to the door, let the student in, find out his name and job.
Continue with:
'May I present Mr/Mrs/Ms . . . the famous . . . Mr/Mrs/Ms . . . did you have a good journey? Would you like a cup of coffee? It's a great pleasure to have you with us today, and I think our first question comes from . . .' Here point to one of the students.
Allow the questions and answers to continue until the new character has been developed. Repeat the process with other students.

What to watch out for: Correct structuring of questions and answers. Either as you go along, make the students repeat the sentence in the right form, or make a note of the general mistakes and correct them afterwards. If there seems to be a student who asks too many questions and monopolises the time, or if there seems to be a student who is content to remain silent, interrupt or make a transition in the process with: 'Excuse me, but I think the lady/gentleman in the corner has a question to ask.'

IV. Possible written follow-ups:
A. Write a letter to a friend describing the person you have just met.
B. Write a character sketch.
C. Write the sketch for a radio play, and then record it.

V. Variation: Pair the students, giving each one a hat. Tell them they are on holiday, on a bus, or in the park, and are sitting next to a stranger. Have the students find out about each other through improvised conversations.

1.10 REGISTER THROUGH ROLEPLAY

1.10.1 PAIRED SKETCH

Age group: teenagers and adults
Level: intermediate to advanced
Time: about an hour
Aim: to enable the students to practise their English orally in a controlled way. To enable the

teacher ... ide the right language and
vocabu... given sketch.
I. Put ... side by side. Ask the students in
pairs ... a short sketch with dialogue (five
minu... setting for the sketch should be
apparen... e manner in which the chairs are
arranged.

dyads set scene for where chairs are

For example:
   in the doctor's waiting room;
   at church;
   at the cinema;
   on the bus, train or plane.
II. Put the chairs opposite each other and follow
the same process.

For example:
   in the confessional;
   at an interview;
   in a restaurant;
   at the doctor's, lawyers, etc.
III. Put the chairs upside down on the floor.

For example:
   a burgled house;
   the beach;
   at the end of a party.

IV. Variations: Use any scenery or props as a
starting point, eg a table, a chair, a clock, an
empty wine bottle, an ashtray with some cigarette
ends in it. Record the dialogue and write it down.
Write the dialogue and then record it.

What to watch out for: During the preparation
period, help the students as much as possible with
their choice of vocabulary and phrasing, so that
the sketches are natural and correct in terms of
language.

1.10.2 THE NOBODY GAME
Age group: teenagers and adults
Level: intermediate to advanced
Time: about an hour
I. One student sits on a chair in the centre of the
group.
II. The teacher, in a clearly defined role, begins a
dialogue with the student.
III. From what the teacher says, the student

should be able to guess what his role is, and to
answer accordingly.
IV. A different student sits on the chair and a
second student is given a clearly defined role by
the teacher. That student begins a dialogue with
the student sitting on the chair.
V. Continue this process until all students have
taken part.

Examples:
   1. You see a beautiful coat in the window of a
shop. You are about to buy it when you discover
you haven't any money.
   2. Go and buy tickets at the cinema.
   3. The heel of your new shoe has broken. Go
back to the shop and change it.
   4. There is an old lady at the other side of the
road. She has been carrying a very heavy suitcase.
Ask her if you can help.
   5. You see an old friend on the other side of the
road. Go over and talk to him/her.
   The students can find their roles in each case.

What to watch out for: The correct use of
language. Correct the students as you go along
and/or make notes for further work later on.
Record the dialogue. Get the group to listen and
get them to pick out their mistakes.

1.10.3 LISTENING DIALOGUES: WORDS TO ACTION
Age group: all ages
Level: lower intermediate to advanced
Group size: five to twenty students
Time: forty-five minutes
I. In pairs, students prepare a *short* dialogue for a
sketch:
   1. in a car—a husband and wife;
   2. in a punt;
   3. in a shoe shop;
   4. in a street asking for directions;
   5. in a pub.
The students are told that they will not be acting
in the sketch, only supplying the voices. The
actions will be provided by another pair, who
know only the most basic details of where and who
they are. As they listen to the dialogue, they
complete the actions.

These dialogues can be prepared at home, and should be corrected before being used in class. Ready-made dialogues, as found in EFL texts, can also be used.

When the dialogues are ready the pair who speak explain the situation to the pair who act and to the rest of the class. The acting pair get into position and decide whose voice each of them will react to. The pair speaking the dialogue read it slowly and clearly. It may be necessary to repeat this process.

Often students will have their own ideas for a sketch. They should always be encouraged to use their ideas and to find something better than the sketch and dialogue they have been given.

Repeat the exercise until all the dialogues have been used.

1.10.4 STARTING FROM A TEXT
Age group: teenagers and adults
Level: upper intermediate and advanced
Time: about an hour

I. The teacher and/or the students prepare one of the skeleton texts before the lesson.

Example:
   P. 'What do you want?'
   D. 'I've told you there's no point in going on.'
(*long silence*)
   P. 'Well, why are you just sitting there?'
   D. 'Oh, for God's sake. Tell me!'
   P. 'Tell you, tell you! Why, just tell me why? Do you listen? Do you care? (*pause*) Leave me alone.'
   D. 'If that's what you want I will.'

II. The sketch is presented in class once or twice. The characters sit in front of the class. The teacher questions the class as to the identity of the characters.

Example questions:
   Are they young?
   Are they male/female?
   Are they related?
   What's the problem?
   What are they doing about it?

III. Discuss the characters, and the several possibilities that arise regarding their situation.

Possible situations:
   girlfriend and boyfriend (perhaps the girl is pregnant);
   married couple (perhaps one partner has found out that the other has been unfaithful);
   married couple (perhaps the husband has lost his job);
   business partners (perhaps an important deal has fallen through).

IV. The characters listen carefully during the discussion but do not join in. When the possibilities have been fully discussed, the students ask the characters the questions that have been raised in class. The characters decide on their identity during the discussion.

V. Through the questioning by the students a story builds up. When the relationship between the two characters is clear, the teacher stops the questioning and leads the students into discussing how the problem could be solved.

Possible solutions:
   They both go and talk to the girl's parents.
   They go to a marriage guidance counsellor.
   They talk to each other honestly and thoughtfully.
   They have a meeting to discuss the next step.

VI. When possible solutions have been suggested, other students take roles and begin a new problem-solving sketch.

Other texts:
A: Do you often come here?
B: I've been here once before.
A: What do you think of it?
B: It's all right.
A: Yes. I know what you mean!
B: How about you?
A: Oh, I'm a regular.
B: Really?
A: Yes, I can't keep away.

A: Have you been waiting long?
B: Long enough.
A: It's always the same.
B: I suppose so.
A: Look at that!
B: I don't believe it!

A: They say it takes all sorts.
B: But there's a limit.
A: It's your turn.
B: Right, thanks.
A: Good luck.

A: What does this mean?
B: You ought to know.
A: If I knew I wouldn't ask, would I?
B: It's a subject I prefer not to discuss.
A: That's typical, but I'm afraid you're going to have to.
B: Are you trying to tell me what I should do.
A: Call it advice if you like, but if I were you I'd take it before it's too late.

An Extract from *Old Times* by Harold Pinter:
Anna: It's quite common to powder yourself after a bath.
Deeley: It's quite common to powder yourself after a bath, but it's quite uncommon to be powdered. Or is it? It's not common where I come from, I can tell you. My mother would have a fit.
(*pause*)
Listen. I'll tell you what. I'll do it. I'll do the whole lot. The towel and the powder. After all, I am her husband. But you can supervise the whole thing. And give me some hot tips while you're at it. That'll kill two birds with one stone.
(*pause*); (*to himself*) Christ. (*He looks at her slowly.*) You must be about forty, I should think by now. (*pause*) If I walked into the Wayfarers Tavern now, and saw you sitting in the corner, I wouldn't recognise you.
   (*The bathroom door opens. Kate comes into the bathroom. She wears a bathrobe. She smiles at Deeley and Anna.*)
Kate: (*with pleasure*) Aaahh. (*She walks to the window and looks out into the night. Deeley and Anna watch her. Deeley begins to sing softly.*)
Deeley: (*singing*) The way you wear your hat...
Anna: (*singing softly*) The way you sip your tea...
Deeley: (*singing*) The memory of all that...
(© 1971 by H. Pinter Limited)

1.10.5 GROUP SKETCH
Age group: teenagers and adults who have already had experience in sketch

Level: upper intermediate and advanced
Group size: six to eighteen students
Time: about an hour
I. In small groups, the students discuss and interpret the meaning of the sketch title.
II. The students prepare the sketch and present it to the class.
Example titles:
   1. A Square Peg in a Round Hole
   2. It All Comes Out in the Wash
   3. A Stitch in Time Saves Nine
   4. A Bird in the Hand is Worth Two in the Bush
III. Sketches for Groups of Three
A. The three of you have been offered a free holiday, but the condition is that you go together. You all want to go to different places, but you have to agree to go to one place or not go at all.
B. The three of you are inside a glass box. None of you knows what is outside. One wants to go outside. One wants to stay inside. You all know that unless you stay together, your lives will be in danger.

1.10.6 FEED, FREEZE AND DEFER
Age group: teenagers and adults who have already had experience in sketch
Level: upper intermediate and advanced
Group size: ten to twenty students
Time: half an hour
I. The students sit on the floor in a circle. Student One stands in the centre; Student Two, and this may be anyone, goes into the centre and starts a conversation with Student One, who must react accordingly. Student Three and/or Student Four join Students One and Two, adding to the improvised conversation in the centre. When the improvisation has been going on long enough or when there are too many people in the centre, Student Five stops the action by shouting 'Freeze.' All those in the centre must freeze in position when they hear 'Freeze.'
II. Student Five may then 'feed out', that is take out any of the students in the centre and/or 'feed in' Students Six and/or Seven. Looking at the positions of those remaining in the centre, Students Six and Seven, whoever is new to the centre, begin a new improvisation. At any time during the improvisation, students outside the

centre, ie. those who make up the circle, may freeze or feed in or feed out.

III. If the improvised sketch is not working, any student can 'defer', that is bring the improvisation to a close. Then everyone goes back to the circle; another student starts out in the centre and the improvisation begins again.

Remember that anyone sitting in the circle may feed, freeze, or defer. Anyone inside the circle, in the centre, must await instructions from those outside the centre.

This improvisation works better when done quickly.

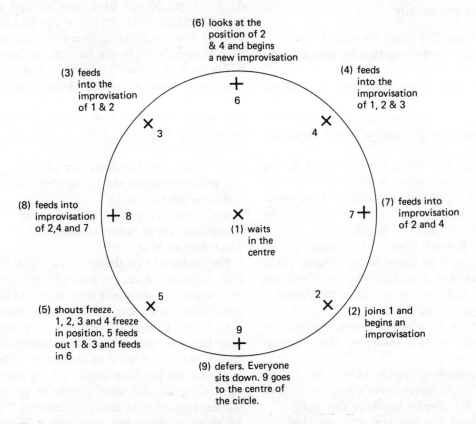

(6) looks at the position of 2 & 4 and begins a new improvisation

(3) feeds into the improvisation of 1 & 2

(4) feeds into the improvisation of 1, 2 & 3

(8) feeds into improvisation of 2,4 and 7

(7) feeds into improvisation of 2 and 4

(1) waits in the centre

(5) shouts freeze. 1, 2, 3 and 4 freeze in position. 5 feeds out 1 & 3 and feeds in 6

(2) joins 1 and begins an improvisation

(9) defers. Everyone sits down. 9 goes to the centre of the circle.

Fig. 4 This is one example of what could happen. However, the varieties are endless and should be controlled by the group.

1.10.7 THE CONSCIENCE GAME
Age group: teenagers and adults who have already had experience in sketch
Level: upper intermediate and advanced
Group size: ten to twenty students
Time: half an hour

I. In fours, students prepare a sketch concerning only two characters in a conflict situation. Students One and Two provide the actions and the actual dialogue between the characters. Students Three and Four speak the thoughts of the characters.

Sample Dialogue:

SHOP ASSISTANT	CUSTOMER
	(*I might have known it would rain if I came without my umbrella.*)
'Good afternoon, can I help you?'	
(*It's nearly closing time. I'll miss my bus.*)	'Um, er. Yes. I was looking for a new suitcase.'
'We have a new range of leather ones.'	
(*I might get rid of him if I show him these. They cost a fortune.*)	'Oh. Ah, yes. Could I have a look at one please?'
	(*Looks as if the rain's letting up.*)
	'Um, er. On second thoughts, I don't think I'll bother after all. I'm in a bit of a hurry.'
'Are you sure? It's no trouble.'	
(*Good. He's going.*)	
	(*I think I might make it to the underground.*)
	'Yes. Yes. Quite sure. Goodbye, and thank you.'
'Goodbye.'	
(*Strange*)	

1.10.8 ROLEPLAY SITUATIONS
Age group: teenagers and adults
Level: intermediate and advanced
Group size: ten to twenty students
Time: preparation time and roleplay about two hours
Roleplays:
 1. Parktown County Council;
 2. Blogg's bequest;
 3. The dam builders;
 4. Green Valley Citizen's Committee;
 5. Fresher City Council;
 6. Trouble at Barker's Bank;
 7. Murder at Rainbow End.

I. Use the plans and maps as comprehension exercises.
II. Give each student a character, making one or two full groups. If there are more students than roles invent supplementary characters.
III. Get each student to prepare himself for the meeting in the role they have been given.
IV. The meeting takes place and a decision is made.

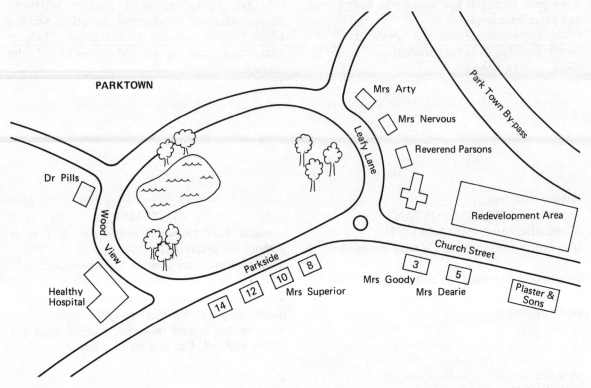

Fig. 5

Parktown County Council

The Plans for the New Centre for Mentally Handicapped Children. The Council proposes the following plans in connection with the new centre for mentally handicapped children:

Plan A

To buy and convert 12, Parkside, the home of the late Mr Aberton. It is expected that the house will be put up for sale sometime in the near future. Negotiations are already under way, as it is not expected that the house, because of its immense size, will attract many buyers.

The house is situated near the hospital overlooking the park, facilitating a liaison between the hospital and the new home, offering the ideal surroundings for the children. 12, Parkside, is a large Victorian mansion with pleasant grounds. The house is known to be in good condition and therefore, the cost of conversion, which is to be undertaken by a firm of local builders, will be well within the sum placed aside for this project. The remainder will therefore be available for any further schemes: for example, an adventure playground.

If this plan meets approval, it is thought that the home will be ready for use by the end of the year.

Plan B

Inclusion of the new centre in the redevelopment scheme which is planned for the old part of the town.

Next year the area adjoining the new motorway will be redeveloped. A tower block, including clinic, sports centre, and covered shopping centre are being considered.

The plans have been under way for some time and the council is under contract to 'Build Big', a large London firm.

If this plan is chosen it will mean that the new home will have every modern convenience and will be planned specifically with the needs of the children in mind. It is also thought that accommodation for all staff will be provided.

As yet not all plans have been finalised as to the date of commencement, and it must be remembered that if Plan B is chosen, the cost of the project will be more than doubled.

Roles

The Chairman—Mr Supercool:

'I must keep the meeting in order at all costs.'

The Social Worker—Mrs Goody, 3, Church Street:

'Number 12 offers an ideal solution to the problem of where to put the new centre. These children are *not* mad. They just have psychological problems. They need to be given a chance.'

The Vicar—Reverend Parsons, The Vicarage, Wood View:

'We must consider the community as a whole and decide with that in mind.'

The Chairman of the Local Arts Council—Mrs Arty, 2, Leafy Lane:

'Well, this is the first I've heard of it, and we've had our eye on Number 12 with the idea of using it as a local arts and crafts museum.'

Mrs Superior, 10, Parkside:

'Am I expected to live next to a houseful of maniacs?'

Dr Stethoscope—The Villa, Blackstable:

'An excellent plan! You can rely on us at the hospital for support.'

Mrs Nervous, 4, Leafy Lane:

'What about my kids playing in the park? Not that I have anything against ... ummm ... errr ... children with problems, but I don't like it.'

Mr Plaster, the local builder:

'Yes, well, it's good business, isn't it? What with the present economic crisis, etc.'

Dr Pills, Greenfields, Woodview:

'I'm in favour of a centre attached to the new clinic.'

Mr News, from the Parktown newspaper:

'This should make a good story.'

Mrs Dearie, 5, Church Street:

'I suppose the new flats will have everything, including vandals. We don't want any new flats.'

STUDENT PREPARATION

In the character you have been given, prepare yourself for the meeting.

1. What kind of person are you?

2. Are you old or young?

3. Where do you live?

4. What's your job?

5. Do you think that mentally handicapped children are dangerous? Give your reasons.

6. Which plan would best suit the children's needs?

7. Which plan would you prefer to be chosen?

8. Do your personal interests conflict with those of the children?

9. Make brief notes of what you want to say at the meeting.

To the Chairman:

Plan the meeting. Make a list of the names of those taking part. Write out the agenda.

Rainbow End County Council—The Bloggs' Bequest

At the reading of Lord Bloggs' last will and testament, it was discovered much to the surprise of the Bloggs family, that Lord Bloggs had left the family mansion and grounds to his hometown.

Representatives from a cross-section of the townspeople have offered the following plans for the use of the house and grounds:

Plan A

For some time now the Council have been considering the possibility of a sports centre in Rainbow End. Since Rainbow End became a London overspill area, sports facilities have become limited, both for the school children and for the population at large. Thus it has been proposed that, as Lord Bloggs was a keen sportsman, his house and grounds should become the new sports centre.

The sports centre will include a covered, heated swimming pool, a gymnasium, a sports shop, a coffee bar, an instruction centre, several playing fields, tennis courts, and a cricket ground.

In order to cover the cost of this project, it will be necessary to sell the house and small garden, although this will not be a problem, as very good offers have been made.

In order to carry out the plans to the full extent, it will also be necessary to cut down the greater part of the forest, leaving a small section, which would protect and give privacy to the house and garden.

Plan B

To take advantage of the historic mansion and its beautiful surroundings by converting the house into a community arts centre.

This will include galleries for art exhibitions, an arts and crafts workshop and showroom where local people could try out their skills and sell their products, a theatre in the medieval hall, and a film club. The grounds will become a nature reserve and bird sanctuary, keeping the natural beauty intact, offering a haven for rare species which may one day be threatened with extinction. The grounds will also provide a learning environment for the school children in the peace and quiet of nature. Some conversion and renovation will be necessary, and it has been thought possible that the cost could be covered by a council loan, which would be repaid in stages by charging an entrance fee. Private donations would be welcome.

Roles

Mr Sporty—the local PE Teacher:
'With opportunities of this sort we'll be able to compete in county events.'

Miss Taptoe:
'My dancing lessons are going very well at the moment, but if there was a sports centre, fewer people might be interested.'

Freda Smith (Née Bloggs):
'I would like to see my father's wishes carried out, but I would also like to see my old home preserved.'

Mr Cine:
'As a man of great experience in films, people would naturally expect to pay a small fee for my lectures.'

Mr Peter Pod:
'The idea of an instruction centre interests me. I could do with a bit of extra cash.'

Mr Cool:
'This meeting is going to be a difficult one, I can see.'

Mr Chopper:
'All them trees'll mean a lot of wood.'

Mrs Wavy:
'It's all too much for me.'

Mr Noall:
'It's a good idea to keep these young thugs off the streets.'

The Dam Builders

In the depths of Scotland, near Perth, flows the River Shin. The river lies in a deep valley. On its left bank runs Perth Road. There are a few houses situated near the river.

Mr Jackson, the engineer, has proposed the following plans for the dam which is to be built in two years' time.

Plan 1

The dam will be built across from Plot Hill to Berth Hill. The mass of water, after passing through the intake conduits, will be directed through Prous Valley. The reservoir will extend to Mr Smith's house, inundating his swimming pool.

Brown's and Callaghan's houses will be destroyed as they will be inundated by the reservoir. Brown and Callaghan will be rehoused in new accommodation to be built on Berth Hill near Mr Punctilious' house.

From the engineering point of view, this plan is the easiest to implement. The project will be financed by a Scottish firm.

Plan 2

The river will first be deviated from Shin Valley into Prous Valley. 1000 feet further on, a smaller dam is planned. The river will rejoin its bed after a few miles. Perth Road will be deviated, and a bridge crossing the dam will join the previous route.

Mr Thin will be obliged to move out, and he is demanding the reconstruction of his chalet somewhere else.

This plan is the most expensive.

Plan 3

The dam is to be constructed a little further upstream than in Plans 1 and 2. The dam will be situated exactly over the site of Mr Smith's house. Mrs Xennon's summer house will be inundated. However, Mrs Xennon is prepared to sell. The water released from the dam will rejoin the original riverbed.

Roles

Mr Yowl:
'The river water is of high quality and very pure. At present, it passes near my house and kitchen garden.'

Mr Wilson:
'I'll fight against any plan which threatens the

position of my house. What happens if there's a flood or an accident?'

Mr Thin:

'I like living where I am, and I see no reason why I should be obliged to move now.'

Mr Brown:

'I think it is in all our interests to preserve the beauty of Shin Valley.'

Mrs Callaghan:

'We must all be reasonable, and consider the best choice for the area, regardless of our personal interests. Besides I've been offered a very good price for my house.'

Mr Smith:

'In my opinion, the first plan has interesting possibilities.'

Mr Punctilious:

'I wake up every morning to a view across hills and valleys, and I have no desire to exchange this for concrete bridges.'

Mr Jackson:

'If the second plan is chosen my business will be endangered.'

Mrs Xennon:

'I came to this meeting hoping to find some explanation. I'm quite lost and I don't understand anything, except that my house may be pulled down.'

Mr Waters—the engineer:

'I feel this is an occasion for me to present the three plans.'

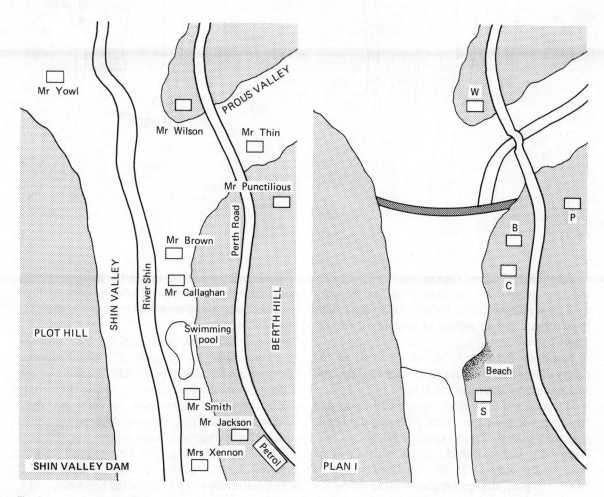

Fig. 6

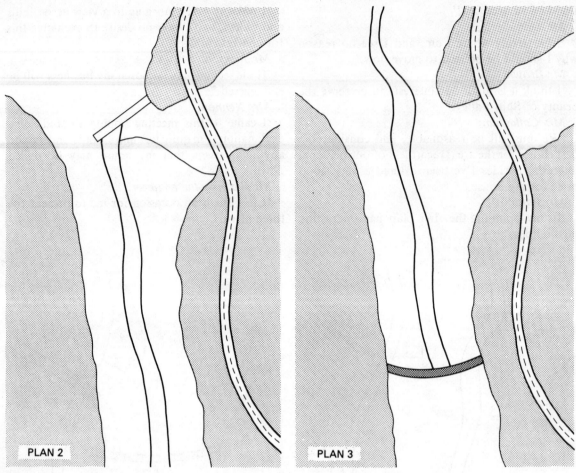

Fig. 7

Green Valley Citizens' Committee

Planning permission has been given for the park land just outside Green Valley. Two plans have been offered and an outline of both plans follow.

Plan A

A luxurious five-star hotel will be built in the centre of this peaceful park land, near the lake and surrounded by beautiful old trees.

The hotel will offer thirty double bedrooms and fifteen single rooms, all with private bathrooms. On the ground floor, there will be a bar, restaurant, and ballroom, all of which will be open to the public. On the top floor will be a swimming pool, the special glass roof enabling the guests to take advantage of every bit of sunshine.

There will be tennis courts in the garden, rowing boats on the lake, and, of course, within three minutes walk, the Green Valley Golf Course.

Plan B

To build self-contained flatlets for old age pensioners who are in need of accommodation, company and independence. Also included in the scheme is an activities centre, offering the people living there the opportunity to carry on their interests and use their talents. Suggestions have included a cottage industries centre.

There will also be a fully trained staff to give medical care and advice, a shop for daily needs, which hopefully will be run by the residents, and a frequent minibus service to the town.

The upkeep of the flats and gardens will as far as possible be maintained by the residents.

Roles

Lord Snooty:

'As you all know, I have connections in high society, and the idea of a luxury hotel for a select clientele appeals to me.'

Mrs Knitting:

'We must care for the needs of our old people.'

Mrs Cake:

'As a home help I'm aware of the needs of our OAP's, moreover, I would be willing to help in any way I can.'

Mrs Smallhead—the Vicar's wife:

'Old people are more religious than rich ones.'

Mr and Mrs Typewriter:

'This town lacks the kind of people we are used to; a hotel of this sort may solve the problem.'

Dr Dragon:

'My reputation as an excellent private doctor would spread far and wide if we decided on this hotel.'

Mrs Niceoldlady:

'More money in the town, more money for my charity bazaar.'

Mrs Venomoustongue:

'Perhaps some famous people will come and stay here. Just think what I can tell my friends about them.'

Miss Study:

'Our charming little town will be filled with pretentious snobs.'

Miss Littlefoot—President of the Citizens' Committee:

'Our small town needs to be developed. The problem is to decide how.'

Fresher City Council

The purpose of this meeting is to discuss the building of a motorway between Pollutionville and Pickup City, necessarily threatening Fresher City.

As you all know, Fresher City was built not long ago, as a health and well-being refuge from the hazards of modern living. Its location, on Pine Forest Mountain, insures an uncontaminated supply of sparkling fresh air.

The town itself offers to its inhabitants and to the many tourists who flock from every corner of the world, the following attractions:

Hot Springs Baths. An underground complex including hot and cold swimming pools, steam baths, a scented plants relaxation room, a gymnasium, and a medical centre. Freshwater Lake swimming pool, out in the open air and situated in a tropical garden, has constantly-filtered waters.

The Park. Surounding the town is a large, beautifully-planned nature park, containing the flora and fauna of the local countryside. One section of the park is covered and simulated sunshine is available there on rainy days.

The Housing Centre. Houses are not more than two storeys high, having been built in a controlled zone centring around Fresher Main Square.

Car Park and Hotels. Just outside the town is a large, good quality hotel and an extensive car park for residents and visitors.

Plan A

Is to build a tunnel under Pine Forest Mountain, running between the Pine Forest and Fresher. Air vents will be placed every three hundred yards, maintaining the level of oxygen in the tunnel.

Plan B

Is to by-pass Pine Forest Mountain.

Roles

Mr Commuter—lives in Pickup City, and often needs to go on business to Pollutionville:

'The shortest journey is the best.'

Mr Channeltunnel:

'With modern science, the risk of pollution is minimal.'

Reverend Revy—from Fresher:

'Think of the human race, and of what we in Fresher have to offer.'

Mr Penny:

'We came to Fresher so that we could live in an unpolluted atmosphere, and we paid for it.'

Mr Towel—manager of the baths:

'I am worried that the vibration caused by heavy traffic will cause structural problems in the underground complex.'

Mr Busy—mayor of Pollutionville:

'We need a road that is quick and efficient, and we're willing to pay for it.'

Mrs Guest—owner of the hotel:

'I have to fill sixty rooms all the year round. People come to take the air. If that goes, they'll go too.'

Mr Tuck—owner of a transport firm in Pickup City:

'They may start the tunnel, but who says they're ever going to finish it?'

Mr Mayor—of Fresher:

'We must fight for our town, but with dignity.'

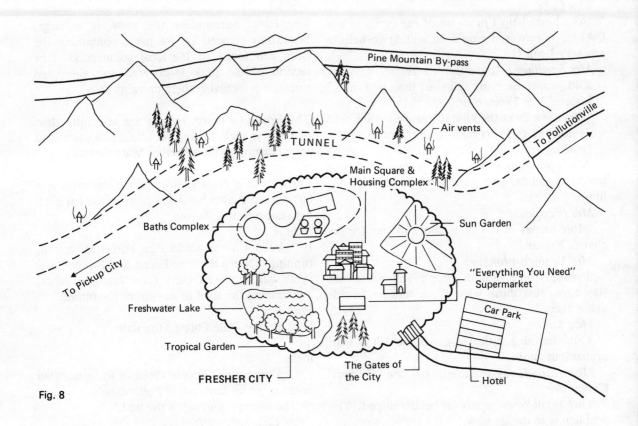

Pine Mountain By-pass

TUNNEL

Air vents

To Pollutionville

Main Square & Housing Complex

To Pickup City

Baths Complex

Sun Garden

Freshwater Lake

"Everything You Need" Supermarket

Car Park

Tropical Garden

The Gates of the City

FRESHER CITY

Hotel

Fig. 8

Trouble at Barker's Bank

Age group: teenagers and adults
Level: intermediate to advanced
Group size: ten to twenty students
Time: preparation and roleplay, about two hours

I. Read the following passage to the students:

'It's Friday afternoon, about 2.30 pm. It's pouring with rain and very cold. You're in town. Perhaps you're doing the weekend shopping or you're working in an office somewhere. Maybe you're at the bank taking out some money, or you have a shop or restaurant and you're paying in your weekly takings.

There are a lot of people at the bank on Friday. You always have to wait a long time, but maybe there's someone you know who's waiting too, and you have time for a chat. Possibly you're working at the bank and waiting for the end of the day and closing time.

Suddenly, three men run in. They have

stockings over their faces and are holding guns. You hear a scream, then there's panic. Everyone starts shouting. You don't know what's happening.

II. Divide the class into the following groups:
   1. bank clerks;
   2. shoppers inside the bank;
   3. shoppers outside the bank;
   4. police
   5. ???.

III. The students fill in the witness questionnaire. The police group or the teacher question the other groups. Each student should add some information to a collective account of the robbery. (Each group may have a slightly different story, but because each witness can only give limited evidence, it is possible to join all the separate information into a general account.)

IV. During the questioning, the students fill in the information table. They then draw and label a plan of the bank.

V. Suggestions
Get the students to write a newspaper article about the robbery.

For advanced students: Get them to read articles from a selection of newspapers, concentrating on the different ways in which a subject can be treated. Ask the students to choose a newspaper and imitate the style in writing about the robbery at Barker's Bank.

TROUBLE AT BARKER'S BANK

Witnesses' Questionnaire

Name:	Was anyone wounded?
Address:	Did anyone escape?
Where were you at 2.30 p.m.	Were the Police efficient?
Occupation:	How much money was stolen?
Describe what happened	Anything else to add?
Describe the three men	

Fig. 9

This can be drawn on the board or photocopied.

Information table

Description of Robbers

	Robber One	Robber Two	Robber Three
Time:			
Date:			
Bank:			
Amount of Money Stolen:			
No. of People in Bank:			
No. of People wounded:			

Fig. 10

Murder At Rainbow End
Age group: teenagers and adults
Level: lower intermediate to advanced
Group size: ten to twenty students
Time: preparation and roleplay, about two hours
The Characters
Lord Bloggs—deceased
Lady Bloggs
James Bloggs—son
Hilda Bloggs—daughter-in-law
Freda Smith—daughter
Ted Smith—son-in-law
Field Marshal Mario Meddle—an old family friend
The maid
The gardener
Inspector Clueless
These characters may be added or the above ones may be changed, according to the group's desires:
Lord Bloggs' secretary
The butler
more police inspectors
The Scene Of The Crime
Rainbow End, somewhere in the South-east of England, a secluded family mansion, deep in the heart of a green, gloomy forest.
The Situation
The Bloggs family, with the servants and one friend, has been passing a peaceful few days at Rainbow End. It is now Sunday morning, and everyone is gathered in the drawing room. Everyone, that is, except Lord Bloggs who is lying murdered in his study, the door to the safe wide open, and the pot of gold nowhere to be seen. The family are awaiting the arrival of Inspector Clueless and the solution of the murder mystery.
I. Read through the text and give each student a character.
II. The students prepare the role they have been given. They must decide on a possible motive. These questions may help them. This preparation can be done in class or outside class.
   What is your name?
   How old are you?
   What was your relationship to Lord Bloggs?
   How did you get along?
   Do you live at Rainbow End?

What do you do for a living?
Do you have any financial difficulties?
Are you married? If so, is your marriage a happy one?
Do you have any secrets? If so, what are they?
Did you have an argument with Lord Bloggs? If so, why?
Was Lord Bloggs' death an answer to your problems? If so, why?
III. The students find out a little about each other in their roles, and as a group (except for Inspector Clueless and any other police) decide on the answers to the following questions:
   What time did Lord Bloggs die?
   What was the murder weapon?
   Who was the last person to see Lord Bloggs alive?
   What time was that?
   Where were you when the murder was committed?
Inspector Clueless: Prepare the questions that you are going to ask the suspects.
IV. Hand each student a piece of paper. On one of these is a mark which will indicate the murderer. The others are blank. This information should be kept secret.
V. The inspector questions the family and other characters in an attempt to find the murderer.

VI. Written work:
A. Get the students to write an article for the local newspaper, the *Rainbow News*.
B. Get the students to write a letter from Lady Bloggs to the Field Marshal.
C. Get the students to write a description of one of the characters.

1.11 INTONATION THROUGH DRAMA
Age group: all ages
Level: lower intermediate to advanced
Group size: five to twenty students
Time: half an hour for each exercise
Aim: to practise intonation patterns

I. INTONATION
Get the students to try to say the word 'sausage' as

many ways as they can. Ask them to find out which differences in meaning the following intonation patterns indicate:

/sausage ._/	agreement
/sausage ._/	question
\sausage .⌒	statement
\sausage .⌒	command
∧sausage .⌒	surprise
∨sausage ._/	disbelief
>sausage ·——	indifference

Get the students to pair off. One student says the word, and the other explains the meaning conveyed by the intonation.

II. PRACTISING PITCH

These can be prepared and then read aloud by each student, by a small group, or by the whole class.

Raise and lower the pitch of your voice:
There once was an old man named Michael Finnigan
He grew whiskers on his chinigan
He cut them off, but they grew againagen
Poor old Michael Finnigan—beginagen.
(Traditional)

An example of a dialogue in a reading passage where a change in pitch helps comprehension:

'The following conversation took place, just outside 9 Park Grove, on Friday, 13 November. Mrs Teeny was just about to unlock her front door and settle down in front of the telly with a nice cup of tea and a fag, when Sergeant Pepper addressed her from his bicycle with the following remark:
"He's done it again!"
"Well I never!"
"We need your help," was his reply.
"Well, I've already told you what my Nancy said. She said it wasn't the end yet and she was right. Bloody marvellous, isn't it?"
With that Sergeant Pepper cycled off down the street.'

III. PRACTISING VOLUME

Start softly and then increase the volume.
Coffee
Coffee
Cheese and biscuits
Cheese and biscuits
Ginger pudding and cream
Ginger pudding and cream
Boiled beef and pease pudding
Boiled beef and pease pudding
Fish and chips
Fish and chips
Fish and chips
Soup
SOU . . . P
(Train rhythm—traditional)

IV. PRACTISING PACE

Start slowly and increase the speed:
A centipede was happy quite,
Until the toad in fun
Said, 'Pray which leg goes after which?'
Which worked her mind to such a pitch
She lay distracted in a ditch
Considering how to run.
(Mrs Edward Craster, *An Animal Anthology*)

V. PRACTISING PAUSE

Pause after each action:
A was an apple-pie;
B bit it; C cut it;
D danced for it; E eyed it;
F fought for it; G gaped for it;
H hung it up;
I inspected it; J jumped for it;
K kicked it; L longed for it;
M mourned for it; N nodded at it;
O opened it;
P peeped in it; Q quartered it;
R ran for it; S skipped for it;
T turned it up; U upset it;
V viewed it; W wished for it;
XYZ all did the same;
And at last the pie was,
By final consent,
Divided among the whole party.
(Nursery rhyme)

Example of a list in a reading passage where correct pausing is necessary to comprehension. Put in the commas and read the passage with pauses:

'On the Bruce Forsyth Show last Saturday night, Mr Twitter won the following prizes:
a pair of nutcrackers wine records two fluffy teddy bears an electric Teasmaid kitchen utensils tools a holiday for two encyclopaedias carpets for the dining room table mats.'

VI. PRACTISING INTENSITY

Stress the underlined words:

There <u>once</u> were two <u>cats</u> from <u>Kilkenny</u>,
Each <u>thought</u> there was <u>one cat</u> too <u>many</u>;
So they <u>fought</u> and they <u>fit</u>,
And they <u>scratched</u> and they <u>bit</u>,
Till, <u>except</u> for their <u>nails</u>,
And the <u>tips</u> of their <u>tails</u>,
<u>Instead</u> of two <u>cats</u> there weren't <u>any</u>.
(Traditional)

VII. READING ALOUD

A. The students bring a prepared reading passage to class.

B. Each student reads his passage while the other students listen carefully and give constructive criticism.

C. While discussing how each student could improve his reading, these hints from the teacher can be included.

1. Sit or stand well and look interested. You will therefore breathe correctly. Your voice will carry, and the audience will have a centre of attention.

2. Briefly introduce what you are going to read. Give author and title.

3. Use the correct volume of sound for the room.

4. Read at the right speed. Avoid the tendency to go too fast.

5. Pause whenever necessary.

6. Raise and lower your voice. Vary the pitch to avoid monotony and to differentiate.

7. Show the important words by increasing the power of your voice.

8. Look at your audience from time to time. Keep in contact with them.

9. Understand what you are reading.

10. Present the spoken word to the audience as the written word has been presented to you.

D. Finally each student re-reads his passage, trying out the ways to improve his reading that have been suggested.

2 *Am I Me?—Roleplay for Intermediate to Advanced Students*

LYDIA LANGENHEIM

2.1 INTRODUCTION

The student learning a second language often finds himself unable to express his personality in the classroom. Resentment can result. This series of exercises, using drama technique, gives back to the student his personality and develops it through his use of English.

2.1.1 WHAT IS 'AM I ME?'
It is a collection of material consisting of:
1. a number of lead-in exercises;
2. a number of planned lessons.

The lead-in exercises are designed to prepare the students and should always be STAGE I of the lesson.

The lessons are designed to help you, the language teacher, to use drama as part of your method. Using it, mime, roleplay, and improvisation will be familiar and natural ways of getting students to communicate.

2.1.2 WHO IS IT FOR?
You will find the material in this section suitable for lower intermediate to advanced students. The oral skill will obviously differ at various levels but the students will be reacting to the same stimuli.

2.2 ARRANGING THE CLASSROOM

The lessons involve the class working individually, in pairs, in groups, and the whole class together, so it is important to create a group feeling from the outset. As far as possible arrange your classroom to suit your activities. Don't let tables and desks create barriers, either use them if the situation requires it, or place them against the wall. Ideally, remember, we don't want a performance area; we want a space where anything can happen. Like this, for example:

Fig. 11

Now try an experiment. Block out the light source in your classroom as much as possible, eg. draw curtains, pull blinds. Put on just one light, then stand in the room and feel the difference in the atmosphere. This atmosphere will help your students, as a group, to feel confident and less inhibited. It will also sharpen the other four senses and improve concentration. If you can get your hands on a spotlight, then students can choose the amount of light which suits them.

2.3 HOW TO USE THESE LESSONS

Before you do any of the lessons, start with one or more lead-in exercises. The exercises under the 'Concentration' and 'Imagination' headings need take no more than fifteen to thirty seconds each. After each exercise you choose to do, get individual students to verbalise their reactions for you and/or each other. A 'relaxation' or 'movement' exercise need take no longer than five minutes. The total lead-in time or STAGE I of the lesson should not exceed ten minutes.

A typical lead-in STAGE I might be:

1. Relaxation—Exercise 1 (four minutes)
2. Concentration—Looking Exercises 2 and 3 (two minutes)
3. Imagination—Exercise 1 (two minutes)

Total lead-in time: eight minutes approximately.

Apart from the 'Commedia', all the lessons can be taught in any order. 'Airport' and 'Emergency Landing' follow each other naturally, but can be taught independently.

The lessons take between forty-five minutes and one and a half hours.

In many of the lessons non-verbal activity precedes the verbal for two reasons:

1. to help the student identify with the role he is to play
2. to cause the student to feel the need for language.

2.4 CORRECTION/RECTIFICATION TECHNIQUES

In these lessons, while your students are working in pairs or groups simultaneously, you have the chance to observe and help with language without getting in the way. The aim is to rectify errors rather than to correct them. Correction holds up the action. Rectifying keeps the action going and enriches the students' use of language. The following techniques are useful:

HOVERING
This means going round the pairs or groups as they are working. Listen for mistakes which get in the way and at an appropriate moment feed in the right form, quietly to the students.

HOT CARDS
Have a number of cards and a pencil handy. Go round the pairs or groups as they are working and, where a mistake is getting in the way, write the correct form on one of the cards. Give it to the student concerned, at an appropriate moment and let him/her decide when and how to use it.

AUDIO/VIDEO RECORDING
Go round the pairs or groups as they are working.

Record sections of two or three of their conversations/dialogues. Remember to note the counter reading on the tape. Errors can be put right by the individual/group/you when the material is played back.

TYPING
If you are a fast typist and the class don't mind the noise, sit behind a pair or group as they are working and type sections of the conversation/dialogue. Use carbon paper so that each student gets a copy.

BLACKBOARD
As for 'Hovering', but write the important errors and corrections on the blackboard instead of saying anything to the student. This has the advantage of anonymity.

2.5 LEAD-IN EXERCISES

2.5.1 RELAXATION
Choose one of the following exercises to prepare the students' body and mind for learning. Simplify the vocabulary of the exercise according to your students' standard and use mime to explain physical vocabulary such as: calf muscle, limp, uncross, relax.

Take the students through the exercise using an intimate tone of voice, remembering you are not drilling the class but inviting the students to trust you. Ideally the students should do the exercise lying on the floor. If some are unwilling to do this, they can do the exercise in their chairs.

Exercise 1. 'Lie on your back...uncross your feet...let your arms lie limp by your sides... Now...close your eyes gently...and breathe evenly and quietly...that's right...think about your toes...breathe in...tense your toes...and relax them...Now think about your legs...make sure your toes are still and your ankles relaxed...breathe in...tense your calf muscles ...and breathe out...relax...let the floor take the whole weight of your legs...the muscles are relaxed and not working...Think about your thigh muscles...breathe in...tighten those muscles...relax them...breathe evenly and quietly...Now your tummy muscles...breathe in...pull in the tummy muscles...tense them... and relax...Now the muscles in your buttocks... tense them...hard...and relax.' Continue in this way until each part of the body has been separately tensed and relaxed. Finish by saying:

'Now breathe in slowly and deeply ten times and with each breath you will become relaxed...alert ...and refreshed.'

Where floor space is limited you can use

Exercise 2. 'Sit comfortably in your chair...let your arms hang loose by your sides...let your head hang so that the chin rests on the chest...close your eyes...let the muscles of your face relax...make sure that your teeth are not clenched tightly together...Now let your shoulders go loose...that's it...and breathe quietly and evenly...As you breathe in you see the colour blue deep and dark...and as you breathe out let the blue fade...to white...as you breathe in your body tightens up all over...as you breathe out the tensions flow away...and fade...and you relax completely...'

Exercise 3. 'You have been swimming and your body is cold...each part of your body feels like ice...As you breathe in your muscles tense... you are rigid and tense and cold...but as you breathe out you begin to let go and relax...The sun is beginning to warm your body...first of all your toes begin to warm and relax...now your feet are warm and no longer tense...'

Continue in this way until each part of the body has been relaxed. You can vary the circumstances of this exercise, eg. drifting in a boat, lying in a hot bath after being out in the cold.

2.5.2 CONCENTRATION

The concentration exercises come under the following headings:

Looking
Listening
Touch
Smell
Taste

After each concentration exercise you choose to do, get individual students or the students working in pairs or groups to verbalise their reactions for you and/or each other.

Looking:
Tell the students:

1. 'Look at your own hand...study it closely...now look at your neighbour's hand and talk about the similarities and differences.'

2. 'Look around the room. How many different shapes can you see? How many different colours?'

3. 'Look at some surface near you, eg. the desk, part of the floor, a door. Look closely at the marks or patterns in the surface and talk about them.'

4. 'In pairs, look at your partner doing something, eg. making a pot of tea, lighting a fire, changing a fuse. Try to copy your partner's actions exactly.'

5. 'Look at the room. Look carefully so that if I ask you to go outside and make a plan of the room, you could do so. Discuss in pairs what each of you has noticed.'

6. 'In pairs, one is A and one is B. A, take a number of things, about eight or ten, from your desk, pocket or bag. Put them on the desk or floor. B, look at them carefully, then close your eyes. A, take away one object. B, identify the missing object.'

Listening: As with the looking exercises, after each listening exercise you choose to do, get individual students or the students working in pairs or groups to verbalise their reactions for you and/or each other. In exercise 5, the sounds can be on tape or imagined.

Tell the students:

1. 'Listen to sounds you can hear inside the room.'

2. 'Listen to sounds you can hear outside the room.'

3. 'Listen to sounds you can hear outside the building.'

4. 'Listen to a moving sound until it is out of earshot, eg. footsteps, a car engine.'

5. 'Listen to three sounds, eg. the telephone ringing, a clock ticking, someone knocking. Divide into groups of three. The first student in

Create a story w/ sounds

each group is to make a telephone sound. The second student is to make a ticking sound. The third student is to make a knocking sound. Make your sounds simultaneously but do not lose your sound or get louder. All groups work at one and the same time.'

6. 'Close your eyes. You are in a cinema. There is no picture, only sound. I am going to make a series of sounds. What is happening in the film?' (Here the teacher makes a series of sounds; door bangs, curtains are drawn, money drops, a high-pitched scream is heard.)

It is a good idea for the teacher to try some of these exercises at home before using them on the class so that you get ideas for other examples. To make concentration more difficult, the following exercises can be introduced, numbers 1 and 2 are best with advanced students.

More Difficult Listening Concentration Exercises
1. Get a student to read aloud a simple passage or give simple spoken instructions, eg. how to cook an egg, how to start a car on a cold morning, how to make a telephone call.

Tell the class to ask him/her irrelevant questions without shouting, eg. What time is it? How old are you? What did you have for breakfast? The student must continue to read or speak.

2. The student carries out same activity but this time he/she must answer the irrelevant questions and then continue reading aloud the passage or giving instructions.

3. In groups of four. One student hums a tune, then the second joins in with another tune, and so on until all four are humming different tunes simultaneously. All groups work at one and the same time.

Touch: The touch exercises are best done with the students' eyes closed. As with looking and listening, after each exercise you choose to do, get individual students or the students working in pairs or groups to verbalise their reactions for you and/or each other.

Tell the students:
1. to feel different surfaces, eg. the material of a skirt or trousers, the desk lid, a hand, hair. Tell

the students to describe and compare these surfaces;

2. to feel the different surfaces of a cigarette lighter, a leaf, a box of matches, a pebble. Tell the students to describe and compare them;

3. to remember the feelings they experience when: they get into bed, are between clean sheets, arm is warmed by the sun, they are crawled on by a spider, they stroke a furry animal. Tell the students to describe and compare these feelings.

Once your class have become accustomed to working with one another and confidence and trust have been established, they can work on physical contact exercises. (Do not attempt this type of exercise if you judge the group to be unready.) Students go into pairs A and B.

Tell the students:
1. 'B stand with your back to A. A, you want B to turn and face you. Make him/her do this without using your voice.

'Now do the same thing again, but this time you can use words.'

2. 'A and B, you are walking together. A, you don't want B to see a person who is coming toward you. Solve the problem without using your voice.

'Do the same thing again, but this time use words.'

3. 'A, you have received bad news. B, comfort A without using words.

'Do the same thing again, but this time use words.'

Smell: After each exercise you choose to do, get individual students or the students working in pairs or groups to verbalise their reactions for you and/or each other.

It is not difficult to bring a few 'captured' smells into class and begin from reality. The smelling should be done with eyes closed. Here are some smells to bring into the classroom: brandy (in a miniature bottle), perfume, tobacco, curry powder, herbs, vinegar.

Ask the students:
1. 'What is this smell? Can you describe it?'
2. 'Go into pairs. You are A and B. When I suggest a smell, A, you tell B what it makes you think of or remember.' (For example: wet paint,

sea air, rotten fruit, gasworks, incense, burning, cigar smoke . . . can be suggested.)

3. 'Remember the smells of your home district. What thoughts come into your head? What do you see?'

Taste: After each exercise you choose to do, get individual students or the students working in pairs or groups to verbalise their reactions for you and/or each other.

A taste of the actual substance stimulates immediate response. Bring to class something like the following: bitter chocolate, mint leaves, sharp sauce, a lemon, salt, water. The tasting should be done with eyes closed.

Ask the students:

1. 'What does this taste like?'
2. 'What do you remember when you taste it?'
3. 'Imagine a taste. How does it make you feel?'

Movement: Expression of feeling exercises
Before asking your students to do any of the following exercises, you can show them how movement expresses feeling.

Mime—waiting for important news or opening a letter which doesn't belong to you.

When you have finished your demonstration, you should ask the students the following type of questions:

'What was I doing?'

'What was I waiting for?' (The teacher must be sure of the answer to this one before he or she can demonstrate anyway!)

'How do you know?'

Get the students to do the following exercises in pairs (A and B).

Tell the students:

1. 'A, you are a doctor. B, you are the patient. Show the doctor you are ill, without using words. Do the same thing again, but this time use words.'

2. 'A, you own a car. B, you are stealing A's car. A, you find B doing this. Do this without using words. Do the same thing again, but this time use words.'

3. 'A, you are walking somewhere. B, you are lying on the ground, badly hurt. A, you see B. Do this without using words. Do the same thing again, but this time use words.'

Imagination: After each exercise you choose to do, get individual students or the students working in pairs or groups to verbalise their reactions for you and/or each other.

— Tell the students:

1. 'Imagine you are: changing a light bulb . . . now mime the action involved. Everyone work at the same time.' (Other examples can be: looking for a lost coin, hanging up a picture, wrapping a parcel.)

2. 'Imagine a jug of water is in front of you. Mime various ways of using it.' (eg. washing with it, putting goldfish in it, drinking it, watering plants.)

3. 'Imagine as you open a door that the room is full of: money . . . chairs . . . cobwebs . . . sausages . . . people . . . books. Mime your reaction to this.'

4. 'Imagine and mime that you are walking on: ice . . . dry leaves . . . eggs . . . hot sand.'

5. 'Go into pairs. In pairs, you are A and B. A, draw something in the air with your finger. B, watch A, and when he or she has finished, copy his or her drawing in the air with your finger.' (The students work simultaneously.)

2.6 CURIOUSER AND CURIOUSER

PRE-LESSON PREP
On a day prior to teaching this lesson—either ask six of the students to each bring a parcel, it must contain something and the contents must remain secret, or bring parcels in yourself.

STAGE I
Lead-in exercises.

STAGE II
Get the class to guess the contents of the various parcels by passing them around, feeling them, smelling them, listening to them. If you have a large class, tell them to go into groups, giving each group a parcel. If the class cannot guess the contents, the parcel is unwrapped. Ask the following type of questions:

How did you feel when you opened it?

What did you expect to find?

Did the shape of the parcel tell what was inside?

Did the contents tell you anything about the person who made the parcel?

STAGE III
Tell the students:

A. 'Get up—you are walking home one evening, alone . . . In the distance you can see a strange object . . . you go nearer to get a closer look . . . on you go. Let me see your reaction.'

Stop the activity after a minute or so. Tell the students:

B. 'Go round the class and tell one another what you found.'

Allow two minutes for this.

STAGE IV
Tell the students:

A. 'Find a partner. You are A and B. A, you find a large box. B, you are sitting nearby. A, you can't move the box. You go and ask for B's help. Do this without words.'

Allow a minute or so for this. Then tell the students:

B. 'Try out that situation again. Take a few minutes to decide the following things.

1. What kind of people are you? eg. impatient, bad-tempered, curious, greedy. Try to play your parts as different people.

2. What sort of box is it? eg. wood, metal, plastic.

3. Who wants to open it?

4. What is inside? eg. something surprising, something shocking, something funny.

5. What do you do with it? . . . steal it . . . eat it . . . get injured by it.'

Allow about five minutes for this discussion. If you think it is necessary, put the questions on the blackboard. Tell the students to act out their 'plays' using words. The pairs work simultaneously. For suggested correction/rectification techniques, see the section, 'Correction/Rectification Techniques.'

STAGE V
Either get a willing pair to show their play to the class or get a spokesman for each pair to report on their play.

2.7 AIRPORT

PRE-LESSON PREP
Write the following four character descriptions on the blackboard. Mask the blackboard until Stage II.

To make organisation as simple as possible, you will see below that the character types are easily adaptable, in role-playing terms, to suit the male/female ratio in your particular group.

Airport Character Sketches
Mr Moneybags:

He is very fond of food and is always talking about himself and what he has just eaten or is going to eat. He likes to play practical jokes.

Miss Goodlife:

She is very attractive and sure of herself. She has no sense of humour, however, and is very impatient.

Mr Clumsy:

He is a very friendly person, but can't see very well. He is always dropping things and tripping over himself. He likes beautiful girls.

Miss Nervous:

She is middle-aged, unmarried and easily shocked. She always thinks she is right, but is a little nervous. She suffers from migraine.

STAGE I
Lead-in exercises.

STAGE II
Introduce the Airport characters from the blackboard. Tell the students:

A. 'Let's find out more about these characters. You are Miss (Mr) Nervous and Mr (Miss) Moneybags. You are in an airport lounge and you've been waiting for the Pan Am flight 521 from New York to Tokyo to be announced. The flight has been delayed. Perhaps you are reading a newspaper, drinking a coffee, looking at the flight departure board, but you are listening all the time for your flight announcement. Now I want you to mime this...go ahead Miss Nervous, Mr Moneybags.'

Stop the mime after a minute or so. Tell the students:

B. 'Go into pairs. You are Miss (Mr) Nervous and Mr (Miss) Moneybags. Miss Nervous, you can't find a seat anywhere. Mr Moneybags, you are sitting on one seat and your hand baggage is on another...Try this out, using words.'

Allow this to continue while there is absorption, then get the students to group around and ask them the following type of question, addressing the student as the character he is playing.

'Mr Moneybags, what did you do while you were waiting?'

'Miss Nervous, why are you so nervous?'

'Mr Moneybags, did you give your seat to Miss Nervous?'

'Miss Nervous, how did you feel when the flight was delayed?'

'Did you show your feelings, Mr Moneybags?'
Tell the students:

C. 'This time you are Miss (Mr) Goodlife and Mr (Miss) Clumsy. Miss Goodlife, you are reading a magazine. Mr Clumsy, you spill coffee over Miss Goodlife. Try this not using words.'

Allow the improvisation to continue while there is absorption, then get the students to group round and answer the following type of questions, as the character.

'Miss Goodlife, how did you feel when the flight was delayed?'

'Miss Goodlife, how did you react when Mr. Clumsy spilt the coffee?'

'Why are you going to Tokyo, Mr Clumsy?'

'Miss Goodlife, how did you pass the time while you were waiting?'

STAGE III
Tell the students:

A. 'Go into groups of three or four. Take five minutes to plan or discuss a little scene involving three or four of the characters.'

After five minutes, tell the students:

B. 'You can act out/try out your scene now.'

For suggested correction/rectification techniques see section 2.4.'

STAGE IV
Either get a willing group to show their scene to the class or get a spokesman from each group to report back.

2.8 EMERGENCY LANDING
PRE-LESSON PREP
Tape the following 'Captain's Announcements' for use in Stage III.

Captain's Announcement I

'Attention, please. This is your captain speaking. Attention, please. This is your captain speaking. I am sorry to tell you that we have engine trouble. We shall have to land at Hawaii. I am afraid this will mean a long delay.'

Captain's Announcement II

'Attention, please. This is your captain speaking. Attention, please. This is your captain speaking. We are going to make an emergency landing. We are going to make an emergency landing. Please do exactly as you are told. Fasten your seat belts tightly. Pull your seats to a fully upright position. Bend forward with one arm across your knees. Place your pillows on your laps. Put your head on the pillow, with your other arm over your head. Push and brace your arms forward. Wait for the moment of impact. You will be warned just before it comes.'

Write the Airport character descriptions on the blackboard (See 'Airport' lesson). Mask the blackboard until Stage II of this lesson or use the overhead projector.

In Stage II there is a listening comprehension. Read it or say it in a quiet, soothing voice.

STAGE I
Lead-in exercises.

STAGE II
Draw a diagram like the one below on the blackboard to help your students arrange the chairs to look like an aircraft cabin. If your classroom makes this difficult, just arrange things as best you can.

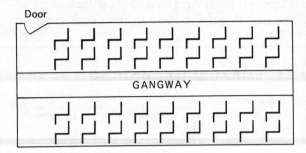

Door

GANGWAY

Fig. 12

Tell the students:

A. 'Go to another part of the classroom... You are in an airport lounge and you are travellers waiting for Pan Am flight 521 which has been delayed. Look at the characters on the blackboard/overhead projector and decide who you are going to be...'

Allow about a minute for this. Tell the students:

B. 'Your flight has been announced, get your things together, check your passport and boarding cards, etc... remember who you are...'

Allow about a minute for this getting into character, then make the following announcement (twice) as a steward/stewardess:

C. 'Will the passengers for Pan Am flight 521 to Tokyo please go to Gate 6 where the steward/stewardess will take your boarding cards.'

Mime the business of boarding cards. Tell the passengers to take their places on the 'plane'. Then once they are settled, say:

D. 'Fasten your seat belts, please. Put out all cigarettes. We are about to take off.'

After a minute say:

'You can unfasten your seat belts. And you may smoke if you wish. We hope you have a pleasant flight.'

STAGE III

Read or say the following listening comprehension as the teacher not the steward/stewardess. Initially you may have to raise your voice to get the student's attention.

'You have been flying now for over two hours. (Repeat, but in a quieter tone)... You have just eaten a good meal... and drunk a nice wine and now you are feeling sleepy... close your eyes... the wine and the food have made you sleepy... The cabin is warm and you can hear the sound of the aeroplane's engines... you are remembering the long wait in the airport lounge... but now you are feeling relaxed and contented...'

Play the captain's first announcement, then tell the 'passengers' to find out what the passengers beside them feel about it. Allow this to continue while there is absorption, then play the captain's second announcement.

STAGE IV

Tell the students:

'You are safe now, the plane has landed. Sit in fours and tell one another how you felt about what was happening.'

For suggested correction/rectification techniques, see section 2.4.

STAGE V

Use the following questions as a stimulus for class discussion.

How many of you were frightened? Why?

Who was sure he or she was going to die?

Did you follow the emergency instructions correctly? If not, why not?

What thought came into your head when you were told you were going to crash land?

Did you want to save anything beside yourself? Why?

2.9 CHARACTER—EYES I

PRE-LESSON PREP

Copy the first two sets of eye pictures at the end of this section (see p. 60 Figs. 14-15).

STAGE I

Lead-in exercises.

STAGE II

Hold up the first set of eyes. Tell the students:

A. 'Look at the picture... Think about it... Now if you had a daughter would you allow her to go

out with him?...' (After a pause, ask individual students to answer this question and to explain their answers).
B. Ask these questions.
'Would you trust this man with a responsible job?'
'Would you trust him with a secret?'
'Would you give him a lift in your car?'
'Would you accept a lift in his car?'
'Would you lend him your car?'

STAGE III
Tell the students:
A. 'I am going to tell you a story... Make yourselves comfortable... Close your eyes... and listen... John Smith was a successful businessman ... He had everything he wanted and he was happy... Then one day his business went bankrupt ... He lost everything... his beautiful house... his expensive cars... his rich friends... nothing left.

For a time John Smith disappeared... Nobody knew where he'd gone, not even his family... but in a small room in a large city... he was living alone and without hope... During the day he stayed in his room and at night he went out to walk the streets... Often he came back to his room late and... drunk... One evening two people come to the street where he is living... John is their brother... They have come to see if they can help him...'
Tell the students:
B. 'Open your eyes. In threes, you are A, B, and C. A and B—John is your brother. C, you are his landlord/landlady. John has not paid his rent for two weeks and you want him to leave. A and B, you are in the street where John lives. You are trying to find the right number. When you find it, you ring the bell or knock. Landlord/landlady... you are watching television.'
Allow the improvisation to continue while there is absorption.
C. Tell the students to group round and ask them the following types of questions:
'Was it easy to find the street?'
'What kind of people live in the street?'
'Was the landlord/landlady polite, helpful, sympathetic?'

'Did he or she ask you in?'
'Did you wait for your brother to return?'

STAGE IV
Show students the second set of eyes. Tell the students:
A. 'Look at this picture... Think about it... Now what kind of mouth do you think she has? Why?' (Address this question to an individual student).
B. 'Go into twos and prepare a physical description of this character.'
Allow a few minutes for this. Tell the students, holding up the second set of eyes.
C. 'This is Mary... she knows John Smith very well—in fact they are meeting tonight... They have something important to talk about.'
D. Get the class to tell you who Mary is—John's wife, boss, daughter... and what kind of character her eyes tell you she is.
Tell the students:
E. 'In your pairs, decide why Mary and John want to meet.'
Allow about two minutes only for this. Tell the students:
F. 'You are Mary and John. John, you are already in the pub. Mary, you are just arriving... Go ahead...'
For suggested correction/rectification techniques, see section 2.4.

STAGE V
Either get a willing pair to show their scene to the class or get the pairs to give a short report back on their scene.

2.10 A FABLE

PRE-LESSON PREP
Make copies of the character descriptions and instruction notes below. Give these to your students at Stage IV of this lesson.

Character Descriptions and Instructions:
Miss Crow:
You are Miss Crow. Your father is a millionaire. You are rich, but you are not beautiful. You are wearing expensive clothes and a very expensive mink coat.

Mr Fox:

You are Mr Fox. You are dishonest, greedy and cunning, but a gentleman.

You are waiting at this International Airport for Miss Crow, a millionaire's daughter, to arrive. You know which plane she is coming on and that she will be wearing one of the most valuable mink coats in the world.

This is your plan. When you see Miss Crow, you are going to tell her you are the fashion photographer of a famous magazine, and that you want to photograph her. You are going to persuade her to take off her coat, which your helper will take away. When he has done this you must get away yourself.

Mr Fox's Helper:

You are Mr Fox's helper, Mr Twoface. You are dishonest, greedy and cunning. You are not a gentleman. You and Mr Fox are planning to steal a very valuable mink coat from Miss Crow, the millionaire's daughter, who will be arriving at this International Airport where you are waiting together. When she arrives you will pretend to be Mr Fox's assistant.

Mr Fox is pretending to be a fashion photographer and he will persuade Miss Crow to take off her mink coat. When she does this, Mr Fox wants you to take the coat and disappear. He will meet you afterwards; but you have decided not to meet him because you want all the money.

STAGE I
Lead-in exercises.

STAGE II
Tell the students:
'Close your eyes and listen. A hungry crow stole a piece of cheese and flew with it onto the branch of a tree . . . She was just about to enjoy the first bite when a fox saw her and called to her . . . Good morning, Miss Crow . . . You are looking very well today . . . How shiny your feathers are! . . . How bright your eyes are! . . . I'm sure your voice is beautiful too . . . Oh . . . If only I could hear you sing . . . just one song . . . I would think of you as the Queen of Birds . . . The crow, who was very vain, believed every word the fox said . . . Flutter-

ing her wings, she lifted up her head and opened her mouth to sing. The cheese dropped to the ground and the fox immediately ate it. He walked away, well fed and very pleased at his cleverness.'

STAGE III
Tell the students:
A. 'Go into pairs. One of you is Miss Crow. The other is Mr Fox. Mime the story. Begin with Miss Crow stealing the cheese.'

Tell the students:
B. 'In your pairs, act out the story using words. Remember, Miss Crow, that you cannot say anything until after you drop your cheese.'

Let this continue while there is absorption, then ask the students to group round. Ask them the following type of questions:

Miss Crow, how did you feel before you stole the cheese? And after?

Why did you listen to Mr Fox and not eat the cheese, Miss Crow?

Mr Fox, what did you say to Miss Crow?

Miss Crow, did you believe Mr Fox's compliments? Why?

What do you really think of Miss Crow, Mr Fox?

Miss Crow, how did you feel when Mr Fox took your cheese?

Mr Fox, do you think you behaved like a gentleman?

STAGE IV
Tell the students:
A. 'Go into threes. One of you is Miss Crow, one of you is Mr Fox, and the third is Mr Fox's helper. Decide who you are. When you have done this, all the Miss Crows go into one group, all the Mr Foxes go into a second group, and his helpers into a third.' Give the appropriate written description and instruction notes to each group. Allow a minute or two for reading comprehension and check that each group understands.

Tell the students:
B. 'Go back into your threes. Mr Fox and his helper, you are waiting in the lounge together and talking about your plan. Miss Crow, go to the bar and get your drink.'

STAGE V
Allow the improvisations to continue while there is absorption. For suggested correction/rectification techniques see the section entitled 'Correction/Rectification Techniques.'

STAGE VI
Tell each three to pair up with another three and compare what happened in their improvisations.

2.11 IMPRISONMENT

The listening comprehension in this lesson requires the students to put themselves in what can be an emotionally 'dangerous' situation. Warn the students of this before Stage II.

PRE-LESSON PREP
Prepare the text in Stage II so that you don't read it to the students, but talk them through the text in a voice which invites trust. If you use a 'Relaxation' exercise from the 'Lead-in exercises' section for Stage I of this lesson, use it immediately before giving the listening comprehension.

STAGE I
Lead-in exercises.

STAGE II
Tell the students:

'You are going to work in threes later on, decide now who you are going to work with ... Now find a space of your own and lie on the floor (sit in your chair) ... close your eyes.

You are lying curled up under a thin blanket ... the air in your cell is damp, your body is sore ... you can't stay in one position for long ... your bones ache ... you are cold. Water drips from the stone walls ... You listen ... The steady drip, drip ... drip reminds you that time is passing ...

Time ... that is all you have left because you are waiting ... Your ears strain to listen and then ... you hear the sound ... footsteps in the corridor ... the key scraping in the lock ... Now you find

yourself being led out into the prison courtyard ... The first rays of the early morning sun make you screw your eyes up ... You shuffle past the row of armed men and ... you flatten your body against the cold stone wall ... every muscle is tense ... your whole body is taut and stiff ... You wait for the order to be given ... nothing happens ... you can't believe it ... slowly you realise your life has been returned ... you ask yourself ... who ... when ... why?'

STAGE III
Tell the students:
A. 'Go into groups of three. In your threes, you are A, B, and C. Decide who is A, B, and C. A, you are the prisoner. B, you are the prison governor. C, you have something to do with the prisoner not being shot. Now, take five minutes to discuss and work out what you think happened next.'

Allow five minutes only for this activity or the improvisation which they are going to do will lose spontaneity. Then, tell the students:
B. 'In your groups, as the characters, act out the scene you have been discussing.'

For suggested correction/rectification techniques, see the section entitled, Correction/Rectification Techniques.'

STAGE IV
Get a willing group to show their scene to the class or get the groups to double up and compare their scenes.

2.12 DESERT ISLAND

PRE-LESSON PREP
Prepare the text in Stage II so that you don't read it to the students but talk them through the text in a voice which invites trust. Have a supply of paper and pencils ready.

STAGE I
Lead-in exercises.

STAGE II

Tell the students:

A. 'Choose partners for later group work in threes . . . Now on your own . . . Find a space on the floor and lie down (sit in your chair). Close your eyes . . . You are lying on white sand . . . on an unknown island . . . The sun . . . is beating down on you . . . from a blue sky . . . that has no clouds . . . Your mouth . . . feels dry and your body is sore . . . from lying for so long . . . You can hear . . . the rush of the sea . . . as it meets the shore . . . and the cries . . . of strange birds . . . You remember now . . . yes . . . it was an emergency landing . . . the aeroplane had to make an emergency landing and you ran from the scene of the crash . . . You can still hear the terrible explosion that followed . . . Now all is still . . . you are here on the sand . . . exhausted, but you are alive.'

Tell the students:

B. 'Go into your groups of three. You have been on the island for two days now and you are the only survivors. You have decided to sketch a detailed map of your island. It is not a large island.'

Give pencils and paper where necessary and allow up to ten minutes for this activity.

STAGE III

Tell the students:

'In your groups, I want you to discuss and decide the following points, making notes where necessary.

How are you going to make use of what is on your island in order to survive?

What kind of "government" is your island going to have?

Are you going to try to escape?'

Allow this activity to continue while there is absorption. For suggested correction/rectification techniques, see the section entitled, 'Correction/ Rectification Techniques.'

STAGE IV

Tell the students:

'In your threes, join up with another group and tell one another about your island and your plans for survival.'

STAGE V—AN EXTENSION

Tell the students:

'In your original groups, mark with an X on your map the location of hidden treasure. Exchange your treasure maps with a different group.'

STAGE VI

Tell the students:

'Now you have a map which shows where the treasure is. In your groups, use the information on the map to discuss and plan an expedition to get the treasure.'

Allow this activity to continue while there is absorption.

STAGE VII

Tell the students:

'Act out the final stages of your treasure hunt.'

All group activity is done simultaneously. A willing group can perform their scene for the class and you can record the dialogue.

2.13 CHARACTER—EYES II

PRE-LESSON PREP

Copy the eye pictures in Figs. 16-21. Put Stage III questions on the blackboard.

STAGE I

Lead-in exercises.

STAGE II

Tell the students to go into groups of three and issue each group with a set of eyes. Allow groups a minute or so to look at the pictures.

STAGE III

Tell the students:

A: 'In your groups, you are A, B, and C. These eyes belong to a missing person. C, you work for Scotland Yard. A and B, you don't know each other, but you have both seen this missing person at different times. The police are trying to build an identikit picture of this person. Other witnesses have agreed that these are the eyes. C, you want information which will make it possible to build the rest of the face. A and B, you can provide this information. C, as well as a description, you want answers to the questions on the blackboard.'

Questions:

Where and when did you see him/her?

What was he/she wearing?

Height/Weight/Special characteristics? eg. a limp

What was he/she doing?

Tell the students:

B. 'Each investigator, that is, C in each group, must have a completed identikit/description of the missing person, writing notes in clear handwriting. If A or B wants to show how the missing person walked/moved/looked, etc., they should get up and do it. Now go ahead.'

Allow activity to continue while there is absorption. For suggested correction/rectification techniques see section 2.4.

STAGE IV

Tell the students:

A. 'C, in each group, you should by now have written:

a clear description of the missing person;

the information from A. Can you give it to me please?'

Re-issue the eyes to the groups, making sure that each group gets a different set of eyes. Re-distribute the information from A.

Tell the students:

B. 'You now have another set of eyes and a report about them.

1. Each of you say who you think this missing person is.

2. Each of you say why you think he/she is wanted by the police.

3. Decide which story is best and be ready to tell it.'

Allow five to seven minutes for this activity. For correction/rectification techniques, see section 2.4.

STAGE V

Choose one or two groups to tell their story to the class.

2.14 COMMEDIA I

In the three Commedia lessons, the characters are stock types taken from the traditional Commedia dell'Arte. The sex of the student playing the part is not important, but obviously ideally the male and female roles should be played as such (see p. 56 for illustrations of the characters).

PRE-LESSON PREP

Write the following Commedia character sketches on the blackboard. Mask the blackboard until Stage II or use an overhead projector.

Commedia Characters

Arrlecchino:

Romantic, has no money, plays the fool, but is clever.

Columbina:

A pretty girl and the daughter of the rich old man, Pantalone.

Pantalone:

An old man who has lots of money, but won't spend it. He tries to keep his daughter, Columbina, at home.

Scapino:

Arrlecchino's friend, a rascal full of ideas and tricks.

Dottore:

He is a doctor and a friend of Pantalone. He thinks he is very intelligent, likes to use long words and likes Columbina.

Beatrice:

She is the beauty of the town. All the young men are in love with her. She is in love . . . with money.

Capitano:

He likes to think he is a brave soldier, but he does not like to fight. He likes pretty girls.

STAGE I

Lead-in exercises.

STAGE II

Tell the students:

'A group of actors travelled around Italy in the early 16th Century, putting on plays in the public squares. These were very simply staged and presented. The main characters were these on the blackboard. The characters developed the story

Arrlecchino

Scapino

Beatrice

Pantalone

Columbina

Dottore

Capitano

and made up a lot of the dialogue and the funny scenes themselves.'

Introduce the characters. Do this by reading the character descriptions on the blackboard to the class. Make sure they understand them.

STAGE III
Tell the students:

A. 'Find a space on your own. You are Pantalone. You are sitting alone in your cold room, counting your money lovingly. Nobody knows you have so much money—'piles and piles and piles of it . . .'

Knock loudly on the desk and then whisper suspiciously, 'Who's that?' Knock again, more insistently and say, 'There's someone at the door, You'd better open it.' The students should respond in character by hiding the money, shuffling to the door and so on. Once they have done this, you stop the mime by saying—'Good, OK. Now let's see what the "Doctor" is doing . . . You are Dottore and you are going to visit Pantalone. What do you need? Get your things together, your coat, your bag of medicines, perhaps a heavy book. When you arrive at Pantalone's house you knock on the door and wait. Nobody answers. You knock again, louder—nobody answers. You become very angry. Go ahead now. You are Dottore.'

Stop the mime after a minute or so and tell the students:

B. 'Go into pairs. In pairs, you are A and B. The A's, you are Pantalone. The B's, you are Dottore. Pantalone, you are in your room, counting your money. Dottore, you are on your way to visit Pantalone. This time use words.'

Let the improvisation continue while there is absorption.

C. Then get the students to group round you and ask them the following type of questions, addressing the student as the character:

'Pantalone, where do you keep your treasure?'

'Dottore, why were you visiting Pantalone?'

'Pantalone, what did you do when you heard someone knock at the door?'

'Pantalone, were you ill?'

'Dottore, do you charge a lot of money for house visits?'

After this short questions time you can introduce Columbina by saying:

D. 'Let's find out more about Columbina. You are Columbina. Arrlecchino has asked you to go out with him tonight, but first you have a lot of housework to do and you have a problem—How can you get your father to let you go out with Arrlecchino. Go ahead . . . mime this.'

Stop the mime after a minute or so. Tell the students:

E. 'Go into pairs. You are A and B. A, you are Columbina. B, you are Pantalone. Columbina, you are going to ask Pantalone if you can go out with Arrlecchino. This time use words.'

Once they have tried out the situation, get the students in their pairs to join up with another pair and compare improvisations. For suggested correction/rectification techniques, see section 2.4.

STAGE IV
Ask the class the following type of questions. Ask three or four different pupils the same question to stimulate discussion and ideas for Stage V.

'What kind of father is Pantalone?'

'Where is Pantalone's wife?'

'Why does Pantalone try to keep Columbina at home?'

'Why doesn't Columbina leave home?'

'Does Dottore visit Pantalone because he hopes to see Columbina?'

'Would you like Dottore to be your family doctor?'

'Has Columbina said to Arrlecchino that her father is rich?'

'Is Arrlecchino afraid of Pantalone?'

'What kind of husband was Pantalone?'

'Does Arrlecchino want to marry Columbina?'

STAGE V
Tell the students:

A. 'Go into groups of three. Make up a short scene with three of the characters. Use dialogue, etc.

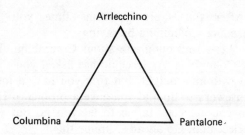

Fig. 13

Allow five minutes for discussion and preparation.

Tell the students:

B. 'Try out your scene now.'

For suggested correction/rectification techniques, see the section entitled, 'Correction/ Rectification Techniques.'

STAGE VI
Either get a willing group to show their scene to the class or get a report back from each group.

2.15 COMMEDIA II

PRE-LESSON PREP
Write the Commedia character sketches on the blackboard (see Commedia I). Mask the blackboard until Stage II or use an overhead projector.

STAGE I
Lead-in exercises.

STAGE II
If you have not already done Commedia I with your students, use Stage II of that lesson before starting Stage II of this one. Remind the students of the Commedia characters by introducing them from the blackboard or overhead projector. Say, 'Let's find out more about Beatrice, Capitano, Scapino, and Arrlecchino.'

STAGE III
Tell the students:
A. 'Ladies, you are Beatrice. You are going out this evening with Capitano. You can't decide what to wear and you have a spot on your chin.

'Men, you are Capitano. You are waiting for Beatrice—striding up and down outside her house—you decide to practise some sword play.

'All of you work at the same time and mime this . . . on you go . . .'

Allow about a minute for this. Tell the students:
B. 'Go into pairs. One of you is Beatrice and the other is Capitano. Beatrice, you are still choosing a dress. Capitano, you are getting impatient outside. When Beatrice arrives you tell her her dress is too low cut and it is too late to go to the opera. Do this without words.'

STAGE IV
A. Let the improvisation continue while there is absorption, then get the students to group round and ask them the following type of questions. Address the student as the character.

'Beatrice, what did you decide to wear?'
'Capitano, does Beatrice always keep you waiting?'
'Beatrice, will Capitano do anything for you?'
'Capitano, do you like opera? Why?'
'Beatrice, do you like to be seen with Capitano?'
'Capitano, does Beatrice have any faults?'

After this short question and discussion time you can introduce Arrlecchino and Scapino. Tell the students:
B. 'You are Arrlecchino. You are in love with Columbina, but her father says you must have money. You are searching your house, hoping to find gold.

'All of you work at the same time and mime this . . .'

Stop the mime after about a minute. Tell the students:
C. 'You are Scapino now. Arrlecchino has told you he needs lots of money quickly. You are trying to invent a machine which will make money. All of you work at the same time and mime this . . .'

Stop the mime after about a minute. Tell the students:
D. 'Go into pairs. You are Scapino and Arrlecchino. You are having a drink of wine together. Scapino, you are trying to persuade Arrlecchino to become rich by taking some of your gold coins. Do this with words.'

E. Allow the improvisation to continue while there is absorption. Then tell the pairs to double up and compare improvisations. For suggested correction/rectification techniques, see section 2.4.

STAGE V

Ask the class the following type of questions. Ask three or four different students the same question to stimulate discussion and ideas for Stage VI.

'What kind of character is Beatrice?'

'Is Capitano free to marry Beatrice?'

'Why is Capitano afraid to really fight?'

'Is Scapino a good friend to Arrlecchino?'

'How else can Arrlecchino get money quickly?'

'Do you think Scapino might advise Arrlecchino against marriage? Why?'

STAGE VI

'Go into groups of three. Make up a short scene with three of the characters. Take five minutes to discuss it and five minutes to try it out.'

You may have to suggest a plot to a group which has no ideas of its own.

STAGE VII

Either get a willing group to show their scene or get one student in each group to report back on their scene.

2.16 COMMEDIA III

PRE-LESSON PREP

As for Commedia I.

STAGE I

Lead-in exercises.

STAGE II

Same as for Commedia I. Omit this stage if you have taught Commedia I or II.

STAGE III

Tell the students to get into groups of seven, then say:

'Sit down. Close your eyes. I am going to tell you a story.'

Read the following story twice.

'One bright morning Arrlecchino is telling his friend Scapino that he has just seen the beautiful Beatrice and that he has fallen in love with her.

'Pantalone is at home counting his money and Columbina, his daughter, is sweeping the floor. Everyone looks out of their window to watch Beatrice passing by. Arrlecchino goes up to her, introduces himself, tells her he loves her, and asks her to marry him. She asks him how much money he has and when he says none Beatrice turns and walks away.

'Columbina has been watching and wants to help Arrlecchino. She says to him, "Why don't we take some of my father's money?" Pantalone is in another room talking to the Dottore, so Arrlecchino and Columbina steal the money.'

'When Pantalone returns to count his money, he finds that some of it is missing and going into the street he bumps into Capitano and shouts at him that he is the thief. Capitano is afraid of Pantalone and does not want to fight him.'

'Arrlecchino runs to Beatrice with his money, but she is going to marry Capitano. Arrlecchino does not want to live. He takes out his heart, throws it away, and dies. Dottore comes along, finds the body and starts to cut it up, but he is frightened away by Columbina. Columbina finds Arrlecchino's heart and puts it back and sews him up carefully. When Arrlecchino wakes up he sees Columbina and knows that she is his true love.'

STAGE IV

Tell the students:

A. 'Use the story you have just heard to make up your own short play, lasting no more than eight to ten minutes. Appoint a group leader.

1. The group leader must write down the cast and the plan of action.

2. Make sure each person knows what he or she has to do.

3. Plan the entrances and exits carefully to give the play order and shape.'

B. Go round the groups, making sure they carry out these instructions. Write the group leader's instructions on the blackboard if you think this necessary.

STAGE V

The groups can polish their improvisations and
write down more of the dialogue. Then they can be
acted simultaneously and/or presented.

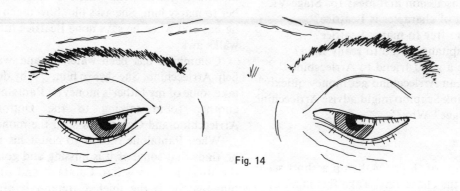

Fig. 14

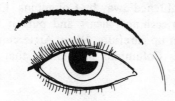
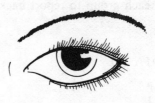

Fig. 15

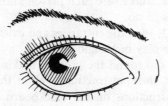

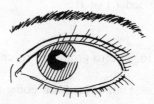

Fig. 16

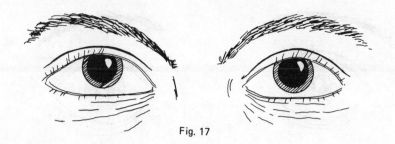

Fig. 17

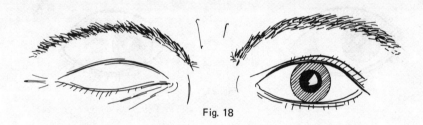

Fig. 18

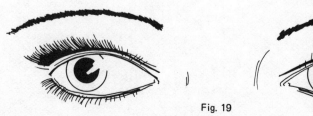

Fig. 19

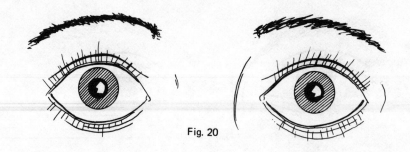

Fig. 20

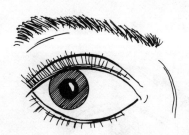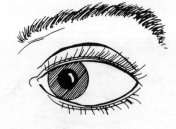

Fig. 21

3 *Music, Music, Music*

LOU SPAVENTA

3.1 INTRODUCTION

3.1.1 WHY USE MUSIC AND SONG?

The activities that follow are based upon the premise that music and song are not rewards for periods of work completed ahead of schedule, not time fillers in the classroom, not purely relaxing techniques, nor are they reinforcement for acceptable responses in the language lesson. There is a need to establish a place for music and song in the EFL classroom. The activities in this section of the book try to show the EFL teacher how to use music and song exercises that will engage both teacher and student in meaningful, real, and honest language activity.

3.1.2 WHO CAN USE THESE ACTIVITIES?

Teachers of English as a Foreign or Second Language and teachers of other languages will find these activities useful tools in their professional repertoire. The student audience is intended to be learners of middle school age and beyond.

3.1.3 HOW DO YOU USE THESE ACTIVITIES?

The activities are divided into two parts: the first—Exercises in Microlanguage—containing traditional language practice activities, with some differences in approach, and the second—Exercises in Macrolanguage—containing humanistic, personal types of activities. The former concentrates on discrete points of language. The latter is concerned with spontaneity, creativity, and the affective sphere of learning.

The purpose of each exercise is given at the head of the exercise. The teacher will also find the preparation necessary, the level of the language learner, and the approximate time of the exercise entered at the top of the page. Most exercises have no need of lower or upper limits on the number of students, but the number of students is discussed where important to the exercise. In the text of each exercise directions, examples, suggestions, and two or three additional songs are given. It is strongly recommended that each teacher choose his or her own songs instead of following the examples contained herein.

3.1.4 WHAT HELP FOR THE TUNELESS?

'I like music. I like songs, but I can't sing, can't play an instrument, and I have no sense of rhythm.' This statement in one form or another serves as explanation for some, alibi for others, as to why music can't possibly be useful in their classrooms. Of course, music and song involve some behaviours which certain teachers might find out of character for them or for their situations. However, there is always risk in real learning, and consequently in fruitful teaching. Decorum may fall. Feelings may show. Talking heads may become whole persons engaged in holistic learning. The gains to be had from the meaningful and thoughtful use of music and song far outweigh risks taken. Teaching is on the brink of personalisation revolution, and the classroom of the future will be distinguished by honest and open communication between teacher and student. Music, in its directness, cuts to the core of expression. Music can be a catalyst for self-expression. However, for those who feel uncertain of themselves, there are ways of reducing such uncertainty.

The teacher can use a record or tape recording. The teacher can use musically-talented or willing students. By doing so, any of the activities in this collection can be approached without reservation.

3.1.5 A NOTE ON USING A TAPE RECORDER OR CASSETTE PLAYER

Here are two generalisations:

1. People who have access to machinery will know how to use it.

2. People who do not have any access to recorders or cassette players probably have enough music in and around them to do without. If you do use a tape recorder or cassette player, make use of the counter on the machine, so that when you look for a song you do not spend minutes clicking back and forth in search. Prepare your tapes so that you will have several exercises in a row on one side of a tape. This will help you to economise on time. However, it is not wise to plan a course-worth of musical activities because you will lose spontaneity, and you will probably go with what is accessible rather than what circumstances and student feeling dictate.

3.1.6 A NOTE OF THANKS AND ACKNOWLEDGEMENT

I would like to thank the people of Korea, Mexico, Saudi Arabia, Yugoslavia, England and the United States for teaching me to sing in different voices. All the exercises in this book did not originate with the author. Teaching is a most fraternal and communal enterprise; when something works in the classroom, the teacher shares with other colleagues. Despite the obvious fact that we borrow from each other in assembling our teaching 'bag of tricks', each of us brings something to an exercise that it did not have before, and pretty soon the 'original' becomes transformed beyond recognition, usually for the better, I might add. The exercises that make up this collection are mine because I have worked with them and revised them, seen them have great effect on my students, and seen them fail. Some of these exercises are 'original' with me in so far as I have never heard of them before, and I created them out of a mixture of teaching problems and imagination. However, it is a curious thing that if one continues reading about new classroom activities for language teaching, one is sure to come across a similar exercise to one one had thought original. That is the way it is. Having offered this explanation of the exercises' provenance, I cannot guarantee pedigree. I also reserve any outrageous or silly statements as my own.

Lou Spaventa

3.2 EXERCISES IN MICROLANGUAGE

The exercises in this section are characterised by their structured nature and by the constraints on the language used and the language possible.

3.2.1 TEACHING A SONG

Some General Considerations: The choice of what song to teach the class involves the following considerations:

1. Does the song relate to the students' experience or does it appeal to their interests?

2. If the song is to revise a grammar point, does it still have interest for the students apart from the structure practice?

3. Does the song appeal to the teacher who is teaching it?

The first consideration is the most important one. If students suggest songs that they wish to learn, the teacher has a greater chance for success in teaching the song than if the teacher simply picks a song known to him.

The second consideration relates to the purpose of using a song. Here the song is being used as a reinforcing device, another way to practise a structure. For example, the folk song, *Turn, Turn, Turn*, by Pete Seeger contains repeated use of the infinitive construction. It can be used after structure practice to provide further listening and oral work. However, the usefulness of the song as a tool for practising structure is proportional to the students' interest in the song. If the students do not really like the song, they will quickly lose interest. The novelty of using songs for practice will quickly wear out if the songs do not have independent interest for the students.

The last question concerns the teacher. Does he really like the song he is teaching? If he does not like it, it will show at some point. If the teacher presents a song that he truly likes, the students will sense this and the enthusiasm of the teacher will transfer to the class.

Presenting a Song: The ideal time for presenting a song to the class depends upon the teacher's intention in using the song. Is the song introducing new language or is it revising language already known to the class? The song has to be integrated into the lesson. It must not stand apart from it. The song can be the centrepiece of the lesson and easily occupy the class for the course of the lesson. However, most teachers will probably want to use the song as one element in the lesson. In this case, the song will serve the function of presentation vehicle, or practice vehicle. In presenting a grammar point, a situation, a function through a song the teacher should begin with a small preparation or lead-in activity. For example, the teacher might ask students to prepare five sentences describing a place in the countryside that they like. Perhaps the next lesson would begin with the students listening to *Country Roads* by John Denver. The teacher would play the song once or twice all the way through. Then he would ask the students to read some of their sentences about places they like and ask them to compare them with the lyrics of *Country Roads*. From this point on the teacher uses the song as he sees fit: perhaps as a catalyst for discussion, perhaps as an exercise in listening, perhaps as a revision of grammar. The skill in using a song as a language learning tool is in keeping the enjoyment of the music and the pedagogical purpose in balance.

3.2.2 RECONSTRUCTING A SONG
Purpose: listening practice and oral practice
Preparation: none
Level: all levels
Time: twenty to thirty minutes

I. The teacher plays a song through once or twice and has the students relax and enjoy the music. Then he plays the song again; this time asking students to listen carefully to the lyrics, making notes if they wish.

II. The teacher asks the students to volunteer words and phrases that they have heard in the song. Without comment he writes them on the board. He then invites the students to link up any of the words that are on the board. For example, this is the first verse of *The Foggy Dew*, a traditional folk song.

'When I was a bachelor, I lived all alone,
I worked at the weaver's trade,
And the only, only thing that I did that was
wrong,

Was to woo a fair young maid.
I wooed her in the winter time,
And part of the summer, too,
And the only, only thing that I did that was
wrong,
Was to keep her from the foggy, foggy dew.'

Let us suppose that among the words on the board are:

lived worked young summer winter
wrong alone

A student looking at these words might recall that 'lived' was linked to 'alone', and so volunteer 'lived alone'. Through this part of the exercise the teacher merely acts as recorder and catalyst. He does not judge and say whether or not the words suggested are the words in the song. After the listing and linking, the teacher directs the class to listen again, trying to identify where the words listed on the board occur in the song, and which words occur before and after the words listed. Furthermore, the teacher might hint that some of the words on the board are suspect, merely by indicating them for special focus during the listening.

III. After this listening the teacher asks the students if all the words on the board are in the song and if so, which words are they linked to. He then asks the students to flesh out the words and phrases by suggesting what the complete lyric lines might be, or what lyrics might fit with the sense of the song. The sentences that the students produce will probably be as close to the lyrics they have heard as they can produce. The teacher should not look for verbatim renditions of the lyrics, but for creative and logical use of the words written on the board. When the students have created several sentences, as much of the lyrics as they can, the teacher should go back and play the song over—this time suggesting that the students try hard to focus on the precise lyrics.

IV. This exercise can easily convert itself into a dictation exercise. The teacher in a song dictation would play the song once through, and then play the song, stopping at the natural pauses in the lyrics as much as possible, allowing students to write down the lyrics they think they have heard. The advantage of this type of dictation is the built-in constraint against subconsciously altering the rate of speech and the natural delivery of the dictation which is a major fault of most teacher-given dictations. Of course, song lyrics are not directly equivalent to normal speech, but then dictation is not a normal writing activity for most people, though it may prove useful in language learning. The point of any dictation is practice in decoding an oral message, and then encoding it in writing. With high level classes, the dictation can turn into a note-taking process. Also in high level classes, the teacher can use the reconstruction exercise to concentrate not so much on structure and lexis as on register, intonation, rhythm, melody, variation and dialect, along with the cultural implications of these.

3.2.3 SONGS FOR STRUCTURE
Purpose: reviewing grammar points
Preparation: previous study of grammar point in song
Level: beginning to intermediate
Time: fifteen to twenty-five minutes

I. After presenting and practising an English grammar point, a song which contains the grammar point can be a very effective method of revising the point.

The teacher should begin by playing the song once or twice in succession. The students are to listen only. The teacher then gives a line from the song and asks the students if they can remember any others with a similar structure. For example:

> As I was going over Gilgarra Mountain
> I met Captain Farrell and his money he was counting
> I drew forth my pistols and I rattled my sabre
> Saying, "Stand and deliver, for I am a bold deceiver".

In this verse from *Whisky in the Jar* the simple past tense and the past progressive recur. The teacher might say, 'Listen to this line, *"As I was going over Gilgarra Mountain."* Is there any other line in this verse like it?' The idea would be to get the students focussing on parallel structures or similar structures in the song. In the case of the past progressive, the end of the second line shows another example of it, this time with the object inverted, ie. *'his money he was counting',*

(OBJECT — SUBJECT — VERB CONSTRUCTION). Further listening to *Whisky in the Jar* will reveal other similar constructions, plus simple past constructions as well, for example, *'I met Colonel Farrell'.*

Additional verses to *Whisky in the Jar*:

> The shining golden coins did sure look bright and jolly
> I took the money home and I gave it to my Molly
> She promised and she vowed that she never would deceive me
> But the Devil's in the women and they never can be easy
>
> Now when I awoke between the hours of six and seven
> Guards were standing round me in numbers odd and even
> I flew to my pistols, but alas I was mistaken
> For I fired off my pistols and a prisoner I was taken
>
> They put me in jail without judge or writing
> For robbing Colonel Farrell on Gilgarra Mountain
> But they didn't take me fists, so I knocked down the sentry
> And I bid a long farewell to the judge in Sligo town
>
> Some take delight in fishing and bowling
> Others take delight in the carriages a-rolling
> But I take delight in the juice of the Barley
> Courting pretty girls in the morning so early.

CHORUS
> Musha ringum duram da
> Whack fol de daddy-o
> Whack fol de daddy-o
> There's whisky in the jar.

After students have listened for the structures to be revised, the teacher asks or gets a student to ask questions using the structure.

For example:
> 'Where was he going?'
> 'Whom did he meet?'
> 'What was Captain Farrell doing?'

This process should continue until it reaches a natural end. The teacher should not prolong it until it becomes drill-like and unthinking.

II. The last step is either learning the song or

retelling the song using the same structures, but changing the narrative a little, by changing voice (from first to third person in *Whisky in the Jar*), paraphrasing and substituting similar lexical items (I was travelling over Gilgarra Mountain. I came upon Captain Farrell. He was counting.

III. Here are three more songs with their grammar points given.

Johnny Has Gone For a Soldier

O Johnny dear has gone away,
He has gone afar across the bay
O my heart is sad and weary today
Johnny has gone for a soldier

I'll dye my dress, I'll dye it red
And through the streets I'll beg my bread
And through the streets I'll beg my bread
Johnny has gone for a soldier

CHORUS
    Shule, shule, shule agrah
    Time can only heal my woe
    Since the lad of my heart from me did go
    O Johnny has gone for a soldier

Structure points—present perfect and future tenses

The Riddle Song

I gave my love a cherry that has no stone
I gave my love a chicken that has no bone
I gave my love a ring that has no end
I gave my love a baby with no cryin'.

How can there be a cherry that has no stone?
How can there be a chicken that has no bone?
How can there be a ring that has no end?
How can there be a baby with no cryin'?

    A cherry when it's bloomin', it has no stone
    A chicken when it's pippin', it has no bone
    A ring when it's rollin', it has no end
    A baby when it's sleepin', has no cryin'.

Structure point—'that' clause, two place predicate with 'give'

Cumbuya

Someone's laughin', Lord, cumbuya,
Someone's laughin', Lord, cumbuya,
Someone's laughin', Lord, cumbuya,
Oh Lord, cumbuya.

Someone's singin', Lord, cumbuya (repeat as above).
Someone's dyin', Lord, cumbuya (repeat as above).
Someone's cryin', Lord, cumbuya (repeat as above).
Someone's prayin', Lord, cumbuya (repeat as above).

Structure point—present progressive

3.2.4 USING CLOZE PROCEDURE

Purpose: listening practice
Preparation: passages with every fifth, sixth or seventh word deleted
Level: lower intermediate and above
Time: fifteen minutes to half an hour

I. The cloze procedure is to delete every fifth, sixth or seventh word from a passage, and then distribute the passages to the class, who must in some way fill in the missing words. They do this based on what they feel will fit grammatically, semantically and stylistically. The teacher can use the cloze exercise as a diagnostic test to see how much English the students have internalised. This can be accomplished by simple distribution of the passage with directions to fill in whatever words they think best. Another way to use the cloze passage is to read it to the students while they fill in the missing words, a modified form of dictation. The cloze passage can be used in conjunction with a song by having students listen to the song and fill in the missing words according to what they hear.

II. The teacher should play the song once or twice before distributing the cloze passage. The students should begin to fill in the missing words when the song is played over again and they have the passage in front of them. The emphasis here is on having students use auditory information to reinforce their notions of what fits grammatically, semantically and stylistically.

If there are no reproduction facilities available for producing the passages, the teacher can simply write the passage on the board and keep it covered until ready to use it.

Here is an example of a song with every fifth word deleted.

My Darling Clementine

O my darling o.........darling
O my darling.........
You are lost and.........forever
Dreadful sorry Clementine
.........she ducklings to the.........

Every morning just at.........
Hit her foot against.........splinter
Fell into the.........brine
O my darling.........my darling
O my.........Clementine
You are lost.........gone forever
Dreadful sorry.........

Ruby lips above the.........
Blowing bubbles soft and.........
But alas I was.........swimmer
So I lost.........Clementine

To be more specific in eliminating words can be worthwhile if one is teaching a particular part of speech or a particular syntactic structure. Taking *My Darling Clementine* again, we will apply cloze deletion procedure to the third verse of the song. See if you can tell what general class of words has been eliminated.

How.........missed.........
How.........missed.........
How.........missed.........Clementine
But.........kissed.........little sister
And forgot.........Clementine

The answer is the category of pronouns. The missing words are: I, her, I, her, I, my, I, her, my. Another benefit of using the cloze procedure in this way is that it offers students a chance to focus on reduced speech in English. For example I can be a fully stressed long diphthong or can reduce to a schwa-sound depending upon how it is sung in *My Darling Clementine*. The point is that the cloze procedure can be used to accommodate whatever aspect of language the teacher wants to focus on.

An alternative to handing out passages with every xth word deleted is to make a recording of a song with the missing words represented by pauses or noises. For example, the student might hear, 'O my darling,.........(Pause) my darling, O my ....(Pause) Clementine.'

Here are the answers to the missing words in the first two verses of *My Darling Clementine* my, Clementine, gone, Drove, water, nine, a, foaming, o, darling, and, Clementine, water, fine, no, my.

III. Here are three songs with every fifth word deleted. The answers follow each song.

Cotton Fields

When I was a.........baby my mother rocked.........in
the cradle in.........old, old cotton fields.........home.
When I was.........little baby my mother.........me in
the cradle.........them old, old cotton.........at home.
Oh, when.........cotton balls get rotten.........
couldn't pick very much........., in them old cotton
.........at home.
It was.........in Louisiana, just a.........from
Texarkana and them.........old, cotton fields at
....
It might sound a.........bit funny, but we.........have
very much money,.........them old, old cotton.........
at home.
It might sound a.........bit funny, but we.........have
very much money.........them old, old cotton.........
at home.
It might.........a little bit funny.........we didn't have
very.........money, in them old.........cotton fields at
home.

Missing words:

   1. little, me, them, at, a, rocked, in, fields
   2. them, you, cotton, fields, down, mile, old,
home
   3. little, didn't, in, fields, sound, but, much, did

Banks of the Ohio

I asked my love.........take a walk, to.........a walk,
just a.........walk down beside where.........waters
flow, down by.........banks of the Ohio.
.........only say that you'll.........mine, in no other's
.........entwine down beside where.........waters flow,
down by.........banks of the Ohio.

.........held a knife against.........breast as into my
.........she pressed she cried, ".........love, don't you
murder.......... I'm not prepared for..........."
And only say that.........be mine, in no.........arms
entwine down beside.........the waters flow, down
.........the banks of the..........

I wandered 'tween twelve.........one. I cried, 'My
........., what have I done? ....killed the only
woman.........love. She would not.........me for her
own.'
.........only say that you'll.........mine. In no other's
.........entwine down beside where.........waters flow,
down by.........banks of the Ohio.

Missing words:

   1. to, take, little, the, the, and, be, arms, the,
the
   2. I, her, arms, my, me, eternity, you'll, other's,
where, by, Ohio
   3. and, God, I've, I, take, and, be, arms, the,
the

O Susanna

O I come from.........with a banjo on.........knee
And I'm going.........Louisiana, my true love.........
to see
It rained.........night the day I.........
The weather was bone.........
The sun so hot.........froze to death
Susanna.........you cry
O Susanna.........don't you cry for.........
For I come from.........with a banjo on.........knee

I had a.........the other night when.........was still
I thought.........saw my girl Susanna.........down the
hill
The.........cake was in her..........a tear was in.........
eye
Said I, I'm.........from the South, Susanna.........you
cry
O Susanna.........don't you cry for.........
For I come from.........with a banjo on.........knee

Missing words:

Alabama, my, to, for, all, left, dry, I, don't,
now, me, Alabama, my
dream, everything, I, comin', buckwheat,
mouth, her, comin', don't, now, me, Alabama,
my

3.2.5 LEAVING OUT SONG LINES
Purpose: making sense of language, fitting
original language to a pattern of rhythm and
rhyme
Preparation: previous practice with cloze procedure
Level: intermediate and above
Time: twenty to thirty minutes
    The teacher records a song with the last line of
each verse missing. The melody should be fairly
familiar or easily learnable. The rhyme scheme of

the lyrics should be fairly conventional, at least for the first attempt with this type of activity. For example, an A B C B pattern as illustrated in *You Are My Sunshine* would be suitable initially. Let the students hear the song as many times as they need to for familiarisation. Usually when the students start humming along to the melody and begin to add a phrase or two to the last lines then they are ready to compose. The students' task in this exercise is to write last lines to the verses of the song. The last line should fit in rhythmically and have the appropriate rhyme scheme. The line should also make sense in the context of the other lyrics. Here is an example:

You Are My Sunshine

	Rhyme Scheme
You are my sunshine, my only sunshine	A
You make me happy when skies are grey	B
You'll never know dear, how much I love you	C
....	B

Obviously, the B line ending in 'grey' is missing its partner in the fourth line, which has been entirely omitted.

A good place to start is with an elicited list of rhyming words for 'grey'. Record these on the blackboard as the students suggest them. The next step is to have them write a complete last line for the song verse.

After one or two attempts with this sort of exercise, the teacher might set the task of supplying alternative lines, as in the following example:

The Sidewalks of New York

	Rhyme Scheme
East side, west side, all around the town	A
....	A
Boys and girls together, me and Mamie O'Rourke	B
....	B

This type of exercise is closely related to the cloze technique, but it is more demanding in terms of original language, sense of rhythm and rhyme, and overall sense of the meaning of the verse. Therefore, it should come after the class has done some practice with cloze technique. Here are three more songs with missing last lines.

Troubled in Mind

Troubled in mind, I'm blue
But I won't be blue always
The sun's gonna shine
....

I'm gonna lay my head
On some lonesome railroad line
Let the 2:19 train
....

Actual missing last lines:

You Are My Sunshine	Please don't take my sunshine away.
Sidewalks of New York	The tots sang Ring-a-Rosie, London Bridge is falling down. Tripped the light fantastic on the sidewalks of New York.
Troubled in Mind	In my back door someday. Ease my trouble in mind.

I Never Will Marry

One morning I rambled
Down by the seashore
The wind it did whistle
....

I heard some fair maiden
Give a pitiful cry
And it sounded so lonely
....

I never will marry
Nor be no man's wife
I intend to live single
....

Last lines:
And the waters did roar.
It swept off on high.
All the days of my life.

Old Smokey

On top of Old Smokey
On the mountain so high
Where the wild birds and turtle doves
....

Sparking is a pleasure
Parting is a grief
But a falsehearted lover
....

They'll tell you they love you
To give your heart ease
And soon as your back's turned
....

Last lines:
Can hear my sad cry.
Is worse than a thief.
They'll love who they please.

3.2.6 REMOVING LEXIS AND LEAVING SYNTACTIC MARKERS

Purpose: to develop the student's sense of lexical appropriateness
Preparation: knowledge of syntactic structures contained in song
Level: intermediate to advanced
Time: twenty to thirty minutes

This type of exercise is designed to develop the student's sense of lexical appropriateness. It is similar to the cloze technique and the elimination of song lines technique in that there is purposeful deletion of elements in the song lyrics. Lexical items are deleted while syntactic markers in the form of morphological markers, words, or phrases are left as they are. The student's job is to write in any lexical items he deems appropriate to the song and its syntax. Lexical clues can be given in the form of certain 'keywords' for the student to build on. The melody and rhythm of the song will also help to give the student ideas about what sort of lexical items will fit. A song in a minor key at a slow tempo probably will not admit words like: 'sunshine', 'blue sky', 'happy day', 'skipping along', and 'bluebird'. Such a song will probably be a bit sad or melancholic, though not necessarily. Here is a song previously used in the leaving-out-song-lines exercise. In this context, it is stripped of most of its lexis.

You Are My Sunshine
You are my sunshine, my only.........
You.........me.........when.........
You'll never.........how much I.........you
Please don't.........

Notice that each blank may or may not represent one word. This should be made clear to the student before starting the exercise. The teacher can help by beating out the rhythm to which the lyrics are set. This will enable the student to play with syllable count and stress in words he chooses.

Here is another song with very little lexis.

Down in the Valley
Down in the valley
The.........so.........
Hear.........
Hear.........

She wrote me.........
She sent.........
She sent.........
The.........

She said that.........
Just to.........
Just as soon as.........
She.........

Down in the Valley is a traditional North American folk song with many versions. Here is one of them.

Down in the valley
The valley so low
Hear the wind whistle
Hear the wind blow.

She wrote me a letter
She sent it by mail
She sent it in care of
The Washington jail.

She said that she loved me
Just to give my heart ease
Just as soon as my back was turned
She loved whom she pleased.

This exercise requires help and clue-giving from the teacher, so that the task does not overwhelm the student. It would best follow similar exercises using deletion techniques, such as cloze exercises, and left-out-song-line exercises. The lexis and structure of the song should be within the learned language of the student, not new language introduced for the first time via song.

One way to make the exercise less demanding is to turn it from an individual to a class exercise. The teacher would ask a class member to act as recording secretary, and that person would come up to the board to write down all the possible missing words as suggested by his classmates. The class would then settle on a version of the song from among the possibilities listed on the blackboard, justifying their choices as they go along.

3.2.7 WORD ORDER

Purpose: to practise discrete listening

Preparation: knowledge of most of the lexis in the song chosen

Level: intermediate to advanced

Time: fifteen minutes

I. Give the students a list of words in alphabetical order. Tell them that they are to find out in what order the words appear in the song. Here is an example using *Auld Lang Syne*.

Partial List	*Auld Lang Syne*
____acquaintance	Should old acquaintance be forgot
____forgot	And never brought to mind
____mind	Should old acquaintance be forgot
____never	And days of auld lang syne.
____should	

The students must listen to the song completely through. The teacher should play the song as many times as the students request him to. However, since the idea here is to listen for the order of single or discrete items in a normal flow of lyrics, the song should be played through from the beginning. If a word occurs more than once, it is the first occurrence that matters for the purpose of the exercise. This should be made clear to the students at the beginning of the exercise.

The answer to the song above is:

    _2_acquaintance
    _3_forgot
    _5_mind
    _4_never
    _1_should

II. The following are three songs with selected word lists.

Whisky in the Jar

____counting	As I was going over Gilgarra Mountain
____deceiver	
____deliver	I met Captain Farrell and his money he was counting
____going	
____jail	I drew forth my pistol and I rattled my sabre
____judge	
____pistols	Saying, 'Stand and deliver for I am a bold deceiver.'
____robbing	
____sabre	
____whisky	

Musha ringum duram da
Whack! fol de daddy-o
Whack! fol de daddy-o
There's whisky in the jar.

They put me in jail without judge or writing
For robbing Captain Farrell on Gilgarra Mountain
But they didn't take my fists, so I knocked down the sentry
And bid a long farewell to the judge in Sligo town.
(Repeat Chorus)

Answers

    _2_counting
    _6_deceiver
    _5_deliver
    _1_going
    _8_jail
    _9_judge
    _3_pistols
    _10_robbing
    _4_sabre
    _7_whisky

In choosing which words to list, the teacher can consider items from the standpoint of lexical similarity, syntactic similarity or phonetic similarity. In *Tom Dula* the words in the list all have the sound /i:/ or /ai/.

Tom Dula

____be	Hand me down my banjo
____cry	I'll pick it on my knee
____die	This time tomorrow night
____knife	It'll be no use to me.
____me	
____my	Hang down your head, Tom Dula
____night	Hang down your head and cry
____she'd	Hang down your head, Tom Dula
____time	Poor boy, you're bound to die.
____wife	

I met her on the mountain
I swore she'd be my wife
I met her on the mountain
And I stabbed her with my knife.

Answers

__5__ be
__6__ cry
__7__ die
__10__ knife
__1__ me
__2__ my
__4__ night
__8__ she'd
__3__ time
__9__ wife

Follow the Drinking Gourd

____bank	Follow the drinking gourd, follow the
____quail	drinking gourd
____river	For the old man is waiting to carry you
____stream	to freedom
____sun	if you follow the drinking gourd
____trees	

Well the river bank makes a mighty
good road,
The dead trees will show you the way
On your left foot, peg foot, travelin'
on,
Follow,
Follow the drinking gourd

Where the great big river meets the little
stream
Follow the drinking gourd
There's another river on the other side,
Follow the drinking gourd

Answers

__2__ bank   When the sun comes up and first quail
__6__ quail   calls,
__1__ river   Follow the drinking gourd
__4__ stream For the old man is waiting for to carry
__5__ sun   you to freedom
__3__ trees   Follow the drinking gourd

The lexical items all relate to nature.

3.2.8 SPLIT SENTENCES

Purpose: to practise listening comprehension and connecting sentence fragments
Preparation: none
Level: lower intermediate and above
Time: fifteen to twenty minutes

I. This exercise is designed to make students aware of how sentences are naturally divided, and to have them practise listening skills. The teacher plays a song through and asks students to listen. He then distributes an index card to each student on which is printed a fragment of a line from the song. The students are to listen to the song and then put together the fragments so that the lyrics of the song are recreated. The teacher plays the song as many times as the students need to listen to it. Here is an example using *She'll Be Comin' Round the Mountain*.

She'll Be Comin' Round the Mountain

1 She'll be comin' round
the mountain   when she comes
She'll be comin' round
the mountain   when she comes
She'll be comin' round
the mountain,   she'll be comin' round
She'll be comin' round   the mountain when she
the mountain,   comes

2 She'll be ridin' six white
horses   when she comes
She'll be ridin' six white
horses   when she comes
She'll be ridin' six white
horses
She'll be ridin' six white   she'll be ridin six white
horses   horses when she comes

3 We'll all go out to meet
her   when she comes
We'll all go out to meet
her   when she comes
We'll all go out to meet
her
We'll all go out to meet   we'll all go out to meet
her   her when she comes

The repetition in *She'll Be Comin' Round the Mountain* makes for a rather easy task. The following two songs are a bit more difficult. In each song in Section 3.2.8 the teacher should read across the two columns for each verse in order to fit together the lyrics.

Stagolee

1 It was early one mornin'   when I heard my
bulldog bark
Stagolee and Billy   were squabblin' in the
Lyons   dark

2 Stagolee told Billy   'what do you think of
Lyons   that
You have won all my   now you spit in my
money, Billy   Stetson hat'

3 Stagolee he went   in the red hot, broilin'
walkin'   sun
Said, 'Give me my six-.   Lord, I want my forty-
shooter   one'

4 Stagolee he went   through the mud and
walkin'   through the sand
Said, 'I feel mistreated   I could kill most any
this morning   man'

Frankie and Johnie

1 Frankie was a good
woman   everybody knows
She gave the tailor a   to make her man a suit
hundred dollars   of clothes
He was her man   but he done her wrong

2 Frankie went down to   and asked for a glass of
the barroom   gin
She asked the   'Has my cheatin' man
bartender,   been in?
He was my man   but he done me wrong'

3 He said, 'Frankie I'll
tell you no story   and I'll tell you no lie
I saw Johnie an hour   with a girl named Alice
ago   Fry
He's your man   but he's doin' you
wrong'

4 Now Johnie he saw
Frankie   and he started to run
Before he got fifty   she shot him with his
yards   gun
He was her man   but he done her wrong

3.2.9 SONG WRITING

Purpose: to use language creatively while following a story line

Preparation: previous work in original writing

Level: intermediate to advanced

Time: thirty minutes

I. The teacher plays a piece of music for the class. The lyrics of the piece should be clear to all and should have some interest for the class. The teacher plays the first verse and then tells the students that they are going to compose a second. At this point the teacher goes over the lyrics of the first verse with the class. He then repeatedly plays a version of the song without lyrics. The teacher emphasises that the students are to write a verse which would make sense after the one that they have heard, and that the verse they write should have a similar rhythm and rhyme to the one they have heard. For example, here is the first verse of *Railroad Bill*.

> Railroad Bill, Railroad Bill
> He never worked and he never will
> They're lookin' for that bad Railroad Bill
> Railroad Bill was a mighty bad man,
> He shot the light out of the brakeman's hand,
> They're lookin' for that bad Railroad Bill

The students hear another verse of *Railroad Bill* without lyrics. The teacher can ease the burden of creating lyrics by supplying the refrain line or some key words.

> Railroad Bill.........the law
> He.........
> They're lookin' for that bad Railroad Bill

Third verse

> Railroad Bill.........died
> ....
> They're lookin' for that bad Railroad Bill

II. Here are two other songs.

The Rising Sun Blues

There is a house in New Orleans
They call the rising sun,
It's been the ruin of many poor boys,
And me O Lord I'm one'

Go tell my baby brother
Not to do.........
Tell him to.........
.........the house of the rising sun

My mother was.........
She.........
My father was.........
.........house of the rising sun

This Train

This train is bound for glory, this train
This train is bound for glory, this train
This train is bound for glory,
If you want to get to heaven then you gotta be holy,
This train is bound for glory, this train

This train don't........., this train
This train don't........., this train
This train don't.........,
....
This train don't........., this train

This train is........., this train
This train is........., this train
This train is.........,
....
This train is........., this train

3.3 EXERCISES IN MACROLANGUAGE

The exercises in this section are characterised by their affective goals and by the lack of constraints imposed on the language generated by the students.

3.3.1 SONG TITLE CHARADES

Purpose: to encourage body talk and mime using words and phrases

Preparation: a bunch of song titles fairly well-known to the class

Level: lower intermediate and above

Time: fifteen minutes

I. Charades is a popular party game in many countries. In this version of the game, there are two teams of students. The teacher gives one person from each team of students a song title. Both students then have about half a minute to read, clarify, and think over the song title. They return to their respective teams and begin to mime the title without recourse to writing or to speech of any kind. The first team to guess the correct title of the song receives one mark. The game ends when one team has reached a preset total of marks, say five or ten. The competitive element can be a stimulus to the performing of the charade because people tend to lose themselves in the excitement of the moment. However, the competition is not to be serious. It doesn't mean anything to win the game. The miming of the song title is the point. In trying to express himself without language, the student must make use of the rhebus principle of using the phonic labels of one idea to establish a phonic context for another idea. For example, suppose the song title has the word 'listen' in it. The student might mime a person looking at or drawing up a list, and then add an action to illustrate one object in another, thus 'list' + 'in' would become 'listen'.

II. The following song titles are from the songs of the Beatles. They are fairly well-known and well-travelled by this time.

Yesterday	*Maxwell's Silver*
I'm a Loser	*Hammer*
Blackbird	*Fixing a Hole*
Good Morning	*Within You Without*
You Won't See Me	*You*
Wait	*I'm Looking Through*
Girl	*You*
Think for Yourself	*In My Life*
Here, There and	*If I Fell*
Everywhere	*I've Just Seen a Face*
The Long and Wind-	
ing Road	

The following titles are a bit harder to mime. They might be reserved for classes who have had practice in doing the easier ones above.

I should Have	*A Hard Day's Night*
Known Better	*Tomorrow Never*
Yellow Submarine	*Knows*
And Your Bird Can	*I'll Follow the Sun*
Sing	*Norwegian Wood*
Magical Mystery	*Back in the USSR*
Tour	
Lucy in the Sky with	
Diamonds	

The songs of the Beatles will work well for young adults because they may very well have contacted English through the songs. For younger classes the teacher need only consult the pop charts. For the more traditional-minded, there is the vast wealth of folk songs in English to choose from.

3.3.2 SONG TITLE STORIES TO PROVOKE BRAINSTORMING

Purpose: to provoke spontaneous language and develop it in written and oral form
Preparation: song titles which are open to broad associations
Level: intermediate to advanced
Time: twenty minutes

The teacher suggests a song title and asks the students to say whatever comes into their minds. The teacher then records these associations on the blackboard and the students write them in their notebooks. The students then use their associations and write one or two paragraphs in their notebooks based on these associations and the images they produce. After they do this, the teacher asks for volunteers to read what they have written to the rest of the class. As class members listen they may comment or question the person reading. Here are some provocative titles from old Broadway musicals.

Born to Dance	*You Never Know*
Damsel in Distress	*Chocolate Soldier*
Fifty Million French-	*East is East*
men	*Hallelujah, I'm a*
Idiot's Delight	*Bum*
Kiss Me Kate	*Joy of Living*
Music in the Air	*Love Letters*
Paris in the Spring	*One Hour With You*
Three's a Crowd	*Queen High*
Fortune Teller	*Desert Song*
Lady Be Good	*I Married an Angel*
Pennies from Heaven	*Million Dollar Baby*
Ready, Willing, and	*On Your Toes*
Able	*Take a Chance.*

3.3.3 INSTRUMENTS: A DISCUSSION

Purpose: to use language imaginatively, to explore stereotypes
Preparation: none

Level: intermediate to advanced

Time: twenty to thirty minutes

I. This is an exercise in putting things together, things we normally don't associate. The teacher should pose the questions below orally to the class or hand them out in written form. In either case, the questions are meant to serve as a catalyst for discussion and composition work. Small groups of students work best in this exercise. The teacher can act as a roving language resource and coordinate the work of each group in a final summary involving the whole class.

Ask the class:

A. What is your favourite instrument? Why?

B. What instrument is most like your personality? Why?

C. Are there male and female instruments? Which are they?

D. Are there instruments fit only for men to play? For women?

E. Identify these instruments with these places:

A	*B*
accordion	Austria
drums	Brazil
guitar	China
gongs	England
viola	Kenya

F. Can you expand this list? What do your matchings tell you?

Each letter is meant to provide the content for discussion or composition. Rather than assigning students to do a particular question, the teacher might suggest that each group decide together on a question or questions.

G. Which instruments are most appropriate:

at a wedding;

at a wake;

at a religious service;

at a dance;

at a government ceremony;

in a child's hands;

in an old man's hands;

in a soldier's hands;

at a rich man's party;

at a meeting of United Nations representatives.

Perhaps appropriate is not the right word for some of these. If you find that you cannot think of which instrument would be appropriate at a certain event or to a certain person, then answer the question as if you were a guide describing what a tourist would see in your country. For example, would he see many children carrying violins?

H. If a man were alone in a deserted place for a long time, would he build an instrument? What would it be like if he did?

I. If you were from one of the places below and there were no instruments because none had been invented yet, what kind of instrument would you make? Why? Out of what materials?

Alaska;

Guatemala;

Japan;

Scotland;

Southern Italy;

Thailand;

Turkey.

J. Look around you in the classroom. Are there any possible instruments? What are they? How would they be played?

K. Which is the largest instrument you know? Who would play it? Which is the smallest? How big an instrument can you imagine? Who would play it?

L. Is there a difference between a noise and a sound? Can one instrument make both? Is there any difference between what happens when a tree falls alone in a forest with no one to hear and when a man cuts it down?

M. Are there instruments that seem to you to fit these ages of man?

infancy;

childhood;

adolescence;

young adulthood;

middle age;

old age.

II. The teacher might want to reorder these questions and to modify them. There is material enough for several different discussions or essays. One or two questions would probably be enough for one lesson.

Another graphic way to involve the students in thinking about instruments and how they relate to people is to have them draw an instrument, any instrument they wish, real or imaginary, and discuss it with the class. This could be restricted to drawing an instrument which best expresses how the students see themselves.

3.3.4 CLASS CHORUS

Purpose: to provide a creative outlet for teacher and class at the end of a course or at any other natural break in study
Preparation: none
Level: any
Time: ten minutes

I. The teacher in the class chorus becomes the conductor of a chorus made up of the students in his class. To start the teacher asks for around ten to twelve volunteers from the class. He then positions them facing the rest of the class. Half of this group will kneel while the other half of the group stands at the back of them. The teacher asks each student in the kneeling group to choose a sound which will belong to that student alone, and which, for him, seems to evoke the experience that he has had in the class. The students at the back are then directed to choose a word each. The word must have a strong association for the student who has chosen it with the activities of the class. Thus the front students who are kneeling each have a sound, and the back students who are standing each have a word. The teacher announces that the chorus is about to rehearse and then takes the chorus through some elementary signals and has each student give his sound or word. After this has been done, the teacher announces to the rest of the class that the chorus is ready to perform.

The teacher then conducts in earnest. The performance is over whenever the conductor ends it. It is important that the teacher really conducts the chorus and that the chorus members respond to directions. In this way the chorus can give a strong indication of student and teacher feeling. It can also yield a good deal of fun for the whole class.

This exercise is most effective when done at the end of a long period of activity, when some sort of summing-up and/or leave-taking is in order. If the teacher uses the chorus more than once with the same class, he might want to hand over the conductor's role to a student.

3.3.5 MELODIES

Purpose: to evoke personal feelings with music and to give students a vehicle for personal expression
Preparation: previous work in personal group interaction activities
Level: upper intermediate to advanced
Time: thirty minutes

I. Play a series of melodies for the class. Each melody should be instrumentally rendered and should represent a distinct style of music. Ask the students to listen once or twice, then direct them to make notes as to how the music strikes them. Ask them to select the piece from among the five melodies that most closely represents them or their feelings.

II. Ask them, 'Which melody is you?' The students should have some time after deciding to make notes and clarify why they have chosen the melodies they have. If the students ask for repeated playings, the teacher should oblige them. When students are ready, ask for a volunteer to talk about which melody he chose and why he chose it. Encourage the other students to listen and ask questions of the student speaking.

III. When the students have talked about which melody they chose then the teacher should ask which melodies they liked and which they disliked. Much of this discussion will have come out before as students differ in their reactions to the melodies. The teacher asks, 'What title shall we give this one?' as he plays the first piece. He directs the students to jot down a title, but not to say what they have written. After playing the five melodies, the teacher goes back and asks for the titles while playing the melodies again.

IV. If the teacher wants to go further, he can tell the students the actual titles of the melodies, and then the students can discuss the differences between the titles they have chosen and the original titles. During the titling exercise the teacher might provoke thought by asking questions like, 'Which instruments are being played?' 'Where does this music come from?' 'Who would you take to a performance of this music?'

V. In conducting this exercise, it becomes important for the teacher to step aside and let the class run itself. The teacher is here to provide a direction when needed. The music is provided to begin personal discussion and expression of feelings. The melodies chosen should be diverse enough to encompass a range of feelings and interpretation. They should be short, about half a minute each in length.

Music is particularly effective in the area of personal expression because it has the effect of crystallising and evoking feelings which would otherwise never surface. In this exercise, students often become involved because they have a personal stake in making themselves understood to their fellow students.

3.3.6 INNER LISTENING

Purpose: to evoke creative use of language, practice listening and communicative skills
Preparation: none
Level: intermediate to advanced
Time: forty-five minutes

I. The teacher is to select three pieces of instrumental music of different types. For example, a classical guitar piece, an Irish jig, and a Japanese koto piece. The teacher plays the three pieces through once and directs the students to listen only. The pieces should each be about two or three minutes long.

II. The teacher asks the students to listen a second time, and at the same time, to jot down impressions that come to mind as they listen to the music. These can be words, phrases, sentences, sounds. After playing the music through the second time, the teacher asks the students to look at what they have written and says, 'Look at your notes . . . Do they fit together? Is there a pattern? Do the words connect somehow? What are the connections between them? Put the words and phrases that seem to connect to each other into a short story. If only some of the words and phrases fit together, then connect those that fit together and forget the others . . . or write two or three smaller stories using all the notes you've jotted down. Concentrate on the possible links between the words you have written.'

At this point the teacher moves back to allow the students time to write. There will inevitably be questions as to what the teacher is driving at. Students should simply be instructed to concentrate on composing short stories based on their notes. One rich avenue for suggestion is to write based on memories of a past experience which the melodies evoke.

After ten or fifteen minutes, the teacher steps back in front of the class and says, 'Read over what you have written. Do you wish to share any of it with someone else in the class? Choose what you wish to tell somebody else. Pick someone to tell your story to.' Here the teacher allows students to pair up freely. He then gives them these directions: 'Now tell your partner your story, relating it to the music. Make sure your partner can retell your story to your satisfaction. Stop when each of you can faithfully retell the other's story.'

III. Then the teacher has one person from each pair of students leave the room. The class will be split into two groups—one inside and one outside the room. The teacher tells each group of students to pair up again and tell their new partners the stories that they have learned from their previous partners. The students must do this in the first person, as if the stories were their own. For example, in telling your partner's story you might begin, 'The music made me feel sad because it was sad and slow. It made me think of a rainy day in Washington when . . .'

IV. The class reforms when the second pairs of students have exchanged stories. The object is now for each person to move around the class in search of the person who has his original story. To do this, the student may only ask questions of the type, 'Were you at the seaside?' 'Was it night time?' 'Did you feel blue?' The exercise ends when each student finds the person who has his original story.

It is important that each student retell quite accurately the story of his partner, and that the partner insist on accurate retelling. If details are shaded over, the exercise loses its power. The exercise works with a class of at least twelve students. Smaller classes will find the last part of the exercise no challenge at all, so it may well be eliminated for small classes, stopping after part three.

3.3.7 SYNESTHESIA A

Purpose: to evoke the language of description, to stimulate talk
Preparation: none
Level: intermediate to advanced
Time: twenty minutes

Choose a large picture that is visible to the entire class. The picture should be rich in evoking images for the student. Then choose three pieces of instrumental music, each one different in style from the others. Play the music for the students, about two minutes for each piece. Ask the students to make associations between the picture and one of the pieces of music that seems to capture the picture best. Let the students discuss their choices and explain them to each other.

3.3.8 SYNESTHESIA B

This is essentially the same as Synesthesia A. However, in this variation the teacher asks the students first to listen to the music and record their associations, and then look at the picture in conjunction with the music. Again the students should write down whatever comes into their minds. The teacher then asks the students to compare the associations they had with each piece of music before seeing the picture and after seeing the picture.

3.3.9 SPINOFF EXERCISES FOR SYNESTHESIA A AND B

Each exercise below will focus on a different skill, but follow from the basic outline of association between picture and music already discussed.
I. Have the students regard their impressions of the three pieces of music as three different aspects of the same picture. For example, let us say that they see a picture of a man working in a field. The students might hear a fast piece of music, a slow, gentle piece, and a mellow, happy piece. The first might suggest the man hard at work, the second, the man at rest, and the third, the man at the end of the day's work.
II. Have the student choose the association that goes best with the picture and develop it into a short essay or story about the picture and what it contains.

III. If the picture contains a person, have the students choose one of the pieces as a catalyst for an autobiography of the person in the picture.
IV. Tell the students to choose one piece of music and work with the associations that it brings to them about the person in the picture. Then direct them to assume the character of that person. How would he walk? Talk? What job would he have? Where would he live? How many people would be in his family? Give the students time to work this out and then set up a situation where all these characters can interact. Each student adapts his personality and mingles with his fellows at a party, at a meeting, at a rock concert, at a trial, and so on.
V. The students could associate the picture and one of the pieces of music to an incident in their lives and outline the parallels.

3.3.10 TOP TEN

Purpose: to have students state and explain their preferences
Preparation: none
Level: intermediate to advanced
Time: twenty minutes

Most students have a radio and listen to music. They know that pop music stations often rate current songs based on popularity and record sales. Have the students come up with their all time top ten list of songs, giving a reason for each selection. The students must also justify why they have ranked the songs as they did. This exercise could easily be given as a homework assignment, so that the following day discussion could begin directly. The top ten need not be pop music, of course, and need not have ten entries. The idea is to get the students talking about why they rank things as they do. The exercise can lend itself to practising the language of comparing and the language of explaining.

3.3.11 SONGS IN MY LIFE

Purpose: to have students talk about significant times in their past
Preparation: none
Level: intermediate to advanced
Time: twenty minutes

I. Have the students list a few very important incidents in their lives that they would be willing to share with the rest of the class. Then ask them if at those important times in their lives, there were songs that were also important to them then. Perhaps, the song is not important in a meaningful sense, but does have a link with the event anyway. If at these times, there were special songs, ask the students why the songs were so special.

This exercise can be assigned for homework so that the students will be prepared to discuss the songs the following day in class.

II. While one student talks about an event in his life and a song that was closely associated with it, other students should be encouraged to question and make comments. The teacher might try asking the class to remember what they were doing at the time of the event the student is relating, and if there were special songs for them at that time.

4 *Teacherless Tasks*

MARIO RINVOLUCRI

4.1 INTRODUCTION

4.1.1 WHO FOR?

Intermediate students of English, ranging from people finishing *Kernels Intermediate* up to Cambridge First Certificate. For classes with shy students, who don't normally say much in the free discussion period. For groups that have just come together and need exercises that improve the group dynamic.

4.1.2 WHAT'S IN THIS SECTION?

This introduction, which includes suggestions on how to use the material, and nineteen tasks.

4.1.3 HOW DO YOU USE TEACHERLESS TASKS?

A. Before you go into class:

1. Choose a task and read it carefully. If there are a lot of words your students won't know, prepare to explain these before the students do the task.

2. Photocopy the page that has the task you have chosen. With tasks one to seventeen you will need about three photocopies if you have a class of thirty, two if you have a class of twenty, and one only if you have around ten to a dozen students.

3. Cut your photocopies up into the slips to be given out to individual students.

4. Be sure to shuffle the slips you are going to give to one group of ten or so students before you give them out.

5. If you have no photocopier available, another way is to copy the text for each student onto small cards.

B. In Class:

The tasks fall into three groups:

1. sequencing leading into problem solving or evaluation—tasks one to thirteen;

2. sequencing and retelling of anecdotes—tasks fourteen to seventeen;

3. question and answer around mystery stories —tasks eighteen and nineteen.

A different methodology is proposed for each of the three groups.

TASKS ONE TO THIRTEEN

(a) Pre-teach necessary vocabulary.

(b) Arrange your students in groups of between eight and twelve. If possible, have each group sit in a closed circle.

(c) Give each student a slip of paper or a card with his or her bit of the task text on it. Depending on numbers of students in the group, you may have to give one person two slips or get two people sharing one slip.

(d) put the following rules up on the board in writing:

> YOU CAN READ YOUR PAPER OUT TO THE GROUP, BUT YOU <u>MUST</u> <u>NOT</u> <u>SHOW</u> IT TO ANYONE.
> DON'T WRITE.
> ONLY ASK ME, THE TEACHER, LANGUAGE QUESTIONS.

(e) Tell the students that their task is to sort out the story situation and to solve the problem it contains.

(f) Sit down outside the circle and make notes of major mistakes that come up. Avoid student eye-contact. At first they may keep turning to you for guidance.

(g) If a circle of students is getting very stuck, you can make a suggestion to them without speaking by writing something on the blackboard —this disturbs their thinking less than when they hear your voice.

(h) The discussion should last between twenty and forty minutes. (Usually, a bit more than half this time is taken up with sequencing the story and the rest is spent working on the problem.)

(i) When the discussion is over you might take

five minutes to put some of the mistakes they have made up on the board and let <u>them</u> correct the mistakes. You should stay mostly silent.

TASKS FOURTEEN TO SEVENTEEN— SEQUENCING AND RETELLING OF ANECDOTES

(a) Pre-teach necessary vocabulary.

(b) Give each student his or her slip of paper.

(c) Ask each person to learn his part of the text by heart.

(d) Check with individuals that they fully understand their parts of the text, and that they have memorised them.

(e) Collect all the slips of paper in.

(f) Ask the students to stand up and move around the classroom. If you have heavy, fixed furniture, get the students to use the front, back and sides of the room. Tell them to try and get into little groups that correspond to their story by saying their part of the story to each other.

(g) When everbody has found the right group, tell them that <u>every</u> <u>member</u> of a group must be able to tell the group's anecdote clearly and adequately. Give them time to achieve this.

(h) Pair students from the different story groups so that they can tell their story to someone who does not yet know it.

NB. In Task Seventeen there is a problem-solving element to be tackled in each group prior to the re-telling phase.

TASKS EIGHTEEN AND NINETEEN—QUESTION AND ANSWER ROUND MYSTERY STORIES

(a) Split the class into two and get one half facing the other half: one half are the questioners and the other half are the answerers.

(b) Give the sentences of the mystery story to four people in the questioner-half of the class. They read them out and <u>their</u> <u>half</u> <u>of</u> <u>the</u> <u>class</u> decides what the best sequence is.

(c) Now tell the questioners that they can solve the mystery by asking the other half of the class 'Yes/No'-type questions.

(d) Give the answerers slips of paper with possible answers on them. If your class is small, each answerer may hold seven or eight slips. If your class is big, each person may have only one or two answers.

(e) The first questioner puts a question to the answer group. The reply may come from anywhere in the group, and occasionally, there may be no answer, or there may be conflicting answers. Do not impose any order on the questioning—let it flow spontaneously.

(f) If the questioning flags after a time, give a gentle written clue on the board.

(g) When the grammar of a question or an answer is wrong, correct it as unobtrusively as possible. A good way is to pass the student a little card with the wrong form and the correct form, for example:

Not: *he didn't goed*
But: *he didn't go*

4.1.4 ADVANTAGES IN THIS FORM OF EXERCISE

A. Since each person has only a small part of the information, he or she is forced to take part in the activity, both receptively and productively.

B. Since fitting together the information is a complex process, the students tend to listen to each other attentively, which is rather rare in the normal classroom situation.

C. As each snippet of information must be clear to everybody, the person reading his slip of paper is forced by the group to try and pronounce clearly. (This is especially the case with Arabs and Japanese when they read.)

D. The students who tend to lead in this kind of task-orientated work are often not the usual cocks of the classroom walk.

E. The members of the group are drawn to focus on each other in some depth—this is often more interesting than focussing on the teacher, who can mostly only have one personality!

F. The flow of discussion is unforced: You will notice one person speaking to the whole group, one person speaking to three or four neighbours, one person speaking to someone across the circle, and sometimes five or six people all speaking at once.

G. In doing these tasks, students learn a lot about text cohesion.

4.2 SEQUENCING LEADING INTO PROBLEM SOLVING OR EVALUATION

TASK 1—THE KISS AND THE SLAP

There were four people sitting in a train in Vietnam in the late sixties.

The four people were as follows: a young Vietnamese who loved his country, an old Vietnamese grandmother, a beautiful young girl of about eighteen and an ugly American soldier.

Suddenly the train went into a tunnel.

There was the sound of a kiss.

All four people heard a slap.

When the train came out of the tunnel, the Vietnamese could see that the GI's face was red.

The beautiful young girl glanced at the soldier and the granny in astonishment.

The granny was asleep in the corner of the compartment.

The young patriot grinned happily.

The problem is: Who slapped who and who kissed who?

Solution
The best solution is that when the train went into the tunnel, the young Vietnamese patriot kissed his own arm loudly and then slapped the GI in the face. Hearing this, the young girl assumed that the soldier had kissed the granny.
   Do not disallow weaker solutions if they seem to satisfy the group.

TASK 2—TELLING THE TIME

Marie went into a restaurant and ordered some soup.

When she had finished she asked for the bill which came to eight francs.

She began counting out the money: 'One, two, three, . . .' and then said, 'Oh, what time is it?'

The waitress looked at her watch: 'Five, Madam,' and Marie went on counting out the francs: 'Six, seven, eight.'

An old man sitting in the corner had been watching this going on. He thought he'd do the same.

He came back next day at lunch time and ordered some soup.

When he'd finished it he called for the bill which came to eight francs.

He started counting out the money: 'One, two, three, . . .' and then said, 'Oh, what time is it?'

The waitress looked at her watch: 'One, Sir,' and the old man went on counting, '. . . two, three, four, five, six, seven, eight.'

How much money did the waitress lose on these two transactions?

Solution
The waitress lost two francs on the first transaction, but she made two francs on the second one, so overall she didn't lose anything.

TASK 3—THE BOSS

The boss lay dead at his desk, his head in a pool of blood.

The police suspected two people: Marie-Lou and Arthur.

They took statements from both.

Arthur said that Marie-Lou said she had killed the boss.

Marie-Lou reported that Arthur said he had killed the boss.

There was only one thing the police knew for sure: one of these two was a <u>liar</u> and the other always told the truth.

The problem is this: Did the police suspect the right people?

Solution
If Arthur is the liar, then what he says about Marie-Lou is false and in the other sentence what he says about himself is also false. If Marie-Lou is the liar, then her report about Arthur is false and what she says about herself is false too.

Therefore both statements must be completely false and the police should be looking elsewhere for their suspects.

Teaching Note
It is essential everybody in the group clearly understands the set of words around the concepts of truth-telling and lying. There are only seven information slips to be given out to the students—this is to make the sequencing easier as some students find this problem hard to grasp.

TASK 4—THE SULTAN
Karagöz was an extremely poor and very clever man.

One day he met the Sultan, who seemed very depressed.

'I can cheer you up,' said Karagöz. 'Did you know I'm the best liar in the whole world?'

The Sultan said he didn't believe it and added: 'I'll give you a hundred gold pounds if you tell me a really big lie.'

'All right,' said Karagöz, 'I'll tell you a bloody great lie, then.'

'One evening your father and mine were playing cards with a group of friends—this was twenty years ago.'

'Your father ran out of money and my father lent him a hundred gold pounds.'

'The sad thing is he never got his money back.'

'You liar!' That's a bloody great lie,' shouted the Sultan.

The problem is: How was the Sultan logically forced to pay up?

Solution
Either way the Sultan Had to pay the money over. If he thought Karagöz was a bloody great liar, then he had to pay him the money for winning their bet. If he said Karagöz was telling the truth, then he would have to pay off his father's supposed debt.

TASK 5—THE ALBATROSS
John and thirteen other men were shipwrecked on a desert island.

As the island was nothing more than a rock in the ocean the men began to starve.

One day John woke up and the others told him that the thirteenth man had drowned.

They also told him that they had trapped an albatross and were going to eat it.

A month later John and the remaining twelve men were rescued.

The first thing John did when he got back to his hometown was to go to a restaurant.

He ordered an albatross stew.

After one mouthful, he got up, paid, and left the restaurant.

The moment he got outside the door he shot himself.

Why did John shoot himself?

Solution
John suspected that what he had eaten on the island was human flesh, not albatross. When

rescued, he checked on this by ordering albatross stew—he then realised he <u>had</u> in fact eaten part of the thirteenth man. This is why he shot himself.

Teaching Note
You may find you need to give a blackboard hint of the kind described in the introduction if the students get stuck after the sequencing phase.

TASK 6—THE AUTHOR

A man went into a book shop and stole a book he'd written.

The next day the author took the book back to the book shop.

He told the assistant that he really didn't like the book.

He asked for his money back.

The assistant promptly refunded the money.

Meanwhile the shop detective recognised the author he had failed to catch the previous day. He arrested him.

When the author's case came to court, he said he was not guilty for two reasons!

<u>He</u> had written the book, so it was <u>his.</u>

He <u>may</u> have taken the book from the shop, but he <u>did</u> bring it back.

The magistrate said that the author was about 10 per cent right, and so he fined him 10 per cent less than he would normally.

The problem is this: Was the judgement a good one? Why or why not?

Solution
The magistrate's reason for thinking the author was 10 per cent right was that he reckoned the author owned 10 per cent of the value of the book, his royalty.

But in fact, the author would eventually get this 10 per cent of the price, which he had pocketed from the book store, back from the publisher.

So the magistrate was quite wrong in his judgement.

Some students may disagree with this solution on the grounds that authors have a right to a lot more than 10 per cent of the price of their books.

Teaching Note
It is important to pre-teach the concept and the word 'royalty' in the specialised sense used here.

TASK 7—THE THIEF

In 1967, a thief stole £10,000 in small coins.

The police caught him, but they had no idea where he'd hidden the money.

The thief was sent to prison for ten years.

In 1970, during his third year in prison, the country changed its money system from pounds to dollars.

Suddenly the prisoner realised that his hidden coins were worthless. They now had no value.

So he wrote to the Home Office and asked them to let him free.

In his letter he gave two reasons. The first was this: He had been sent to prison for ten years for stealing £10,000, <u>not</u> for stealing worthless coins.

His second point was this: They had been right to send him to prison in 1967, but they would now be wrong to keep him there.

The Home Office let him go free.

Do you think the Home Office was right or wrong?

Solution
Legally-minded students usually feel the Home Office was wrong, because the man was sent to

prison for what he did in 1967—they say what happened since doesn't matter.

A minority of students seem to agree with the prisoner's case that it is wrong for him to spend seven further years in jail for what now turns out to have become minor pilfering.

TASK 8—THE BET

Henry bet his friends he was brave enough to spend the whole night locked up alone in a room with a dead body.

One moonlit night they took him to a house lost in the Scottish mountains. It was said to be haunted.

Henry and his friends crept up the creaking stairs and entered a moonlit room.

In the room they saw what looked like a corpse.

It was slumped across the table in the middle of the room, a girl's body with long black hair.

Henry heard the key turn twice in the lock as his friends left him—he was alone in the moonlit room with the body, all alone.

They came back at first light next day; they unlocked the door and suddenly saw that two terrible things had happened:

He was dead.

She was sitting looking out of the window, mumbling crazily to herself.

And as she mumbled she passed her hand distractedly through her snow-white hair.

Can you work out what happened that night in the locked room?

Solution

Henry's friends had persuaded the dark-haired girl to act the part of a corpse in the haunted house. She found it impossible to keep absolutely still and Henry saw her move. Scared out of his mind, he had a heart-attack and died.

The girl was horrified at what had happened—her hair turned white and for a time she went half crazy.

TASK 9—A QUESTION OF WASHING

This whole story took place in the 1930s.

Two girls were sitting in a train carriage.

Theirs was the one nearest the engine.

This was a steam locomotive and it had clouds of black smoke belching from its funnel.

Forget the engine and come back to the girls in the carriage—they were sitting by the window, facing each other.

Now that you understand where the girls were and what sort of train it was, let me tell you what happened: the train rushed into a tunnel.

It was a long one and the train took three minutes to get through it.

When they were out in the daylight again, one of the girls went and washed her face.

She needed to much less than the other.

Which one went to wash her face and why?

Solution

When they came out of the tunnel the girl sitting with her back to the engine saw that the other girl had a very dirty face, so she went off to wash her own, thinking it was the same. The girl with the very dirty face, who had been sitting facing the engine, didn't feel the need to wash her face because her friend's was comparatively clean.

TASK 10—THE BARBERS

A philosopher went to visit a small town lost in an immense desert.

On arrival he decided that he rather badly needed

a haircut and asked if there were any barbers in this town.

There were two, he was told.

He was also told that the first was a very smart man with excellently cut hair and a very clean shop.

The second wore dirty clothes and his place was in a real mess. What's more, his hair was horribly badly cut.

Neither the first nor the second had an assistant.

After hearing about the two barbers, the wise man wondered which of them to go to.

As he couldn't immediately make up his mind, he went and sat under a tree to think the problem through.

After thirty seconds thought, he jumped to his feet and strode across the square to one of the barbers' shops.

Your problem is this: which one did he go to and why was he sure he was right?

Solution
Since the town was in a vast desert and since the two barbers had no assistants, the dirty one must cut the clean one's hair, and vice-versa. Therefore, the dirty one was a good barber and the clean one hopeless.

TASK 11—A SAD STORY

Jim's wife had just walked out on him.

He rushed out of the home, pedalled unsteadily to the local and started drinking.

A couple of hours later, he staggered out of the pub and somehow got on his bike.

He was wobbling from side to side down the High Street when a car knocked him down, crushing his leg.

The driver went straight on without slowing down at all.

He was rushing his wife to the maternity hospital.

When they finally got Jim to hospital, he had to wait three hours in casualty.

The houseman who finally examined him, amputated the wrong leg.

This doctor had been on duty for over 27 hours.

There are five people in the story—each of you take a piece of paper and rank the five people in your own individual order of moral preference. Be ready to explain why to the rest of the group.

Solution
There is no logical one—it's up to each person's moral judgement.

Teaching Note
This lesson will fall naturally into three phases:
1. group sequencing;
2. jotting down a ranking order, with each student working individually;
3. individuals reading out their rankings and explaining them to the others.

TASK 12—ABORTION

Mary's husband had been away abroad for six months. But Mary was not lonely—her boyfriend John saw to this.

Suddenly Mary realised she was pregnant—she told John and asked him what she should do. He said she should do exactly what she wanted—nothing to do with him.

As Mary had been given a strong religious upbringing, she felt guilty about having an abortion. She rang up a priest—he told her bluntly that abortion was murder.

After talking to the priest, she waited another two weeks. Then she went to her family doctor, a woman. The doctor told her she could perfectly well have the child—she refused her a free National Health abortion.

Being short of money, Mary borrowed some from her brother and told him what she wanted it for.

She then had a private abortion, for which a fat consultant charged her £250.

She paid her brother the money back, but he then started blackmailing her for further sums—he threatened to tell Mary's husband all that had happened.

The husband got back and found out from a neighbour about Mary's boyfriend and her abortion. He decided to go on living with her because he was afraid of a scandal if he left her.

There are seven people in the story—each of you take a piece of paper and rank the seven people in your own individual order of moral preference. Be ready to justify your ranking to the rest of the group.

Solution
See Task Eleven.

Teaching Notes
See Task Eleven.

TASK 13—THE LAWNMOWER

Are you tired of pushing a back-breaking hand mower? Well, we have just the thing for you.

So you usually can't get the thing started? Ours never gives us any trouble on that score.

Yours noisy? Disturbs the neighbours on a Sunday afternoon? Ours is nearly always silent.

Do you dislike the fumes from your present machine? We propose a solution that solves all the problems of pollution.

No petrol fumes, no dangerous electric wires, in fact, no work at all for you—our great new market innovation is fully automated.

Never needs oiling.

There is no way you can catch your fingers in its wheels.

The model we present to you now is a logical evolution from much earlier models.

Our product's colour scheme blends with your garden—purely natural colours.

The problem is this: What exactly is this lawn mowing innovation?

Solution
A sheep, or any other herbivorous animal.

Teaching Note
If the students come to this riddle after tackling some of the earlier tasks, they will probably try to sequence their sentences.

   If, after a time, they fail to work out that this is unnecessary, you may decide to give them a blackboard prompt of the sort mentioned in the introduction.

4.3 SEQUENCING AND RE-TELLING TWO OR MORE STORIES

TASK 14—THREE JOKES

'That shirt I bought has a hole in it—I want my money back.'

'I'm sorry I can't give your money back. I never give refunds.'

'But look at that notice in your window: it says: 'Money refunded if not satisfactory.'

'Sure, but the money you gave me was very satisfactory.'

'Are you going to pay me what you owe me?' said the creditor to the debtor.

'Not just yet,' replied the other.

'If you don't pay me back, I'll tell all your other creditors that you did pay me back.'

'When I was your age,' said the father, 'I worked sixteen hours a day to learn the business.'

'Good thing too. If you hadn't, I might have had to do the same.'

TASK 15—THE CHAIRPERSON AND THE WINDOW

The board chairperson lost her temper and screamed:

'Half of you people are complete idiots!'

At this one of the directors took offence:

'I feel you should withdraw that remark,' he suggested tersely.

The chairperson thought for a moment:

'All right, I apologise—at least 50 per cent of the people present in this room are not idiots!'

'It's cold outside,' he grumbled.

She took no notice of him.

'You know, it's really cold outside, dear,' he said again.

Finally she leapt out of bed and slammed the window shut.

'So now it's warm outside!' she said, pulling the covers back over her head.

TASK 16—TWO STORIES ABOUT LANGUAGE

John had come to France to learn the language.

His teacher said to the group: 'You've been here three weeks now—has anybody started dreaming in French?'

John answered: 'Yes, me—I had a dream in French last night.'

'What was it about?'

'No idea, I couldn't understand a word of it!'

John, who was seven, came from a Breton-speaking community in western France.

But at school he was only allowed to speak French.

On the first day of school the teacher caught John disobeying this rule.

He told him he would be beaten at the end of school unless he reported another boy or girl for doing the same thing.

Then the other child would get the beating, instead of John, the teacher said.

This way the children soon stopped using their native language and only used French.

Teaching Note
After re-telling in pairs you might put up the following instructions on the board:
A. Write down three words to describe the way the Breton children were forced to speak French.
B. Did you have to change your speech when you first went to school? If so, how did you feel?
C. Is dreaming or not dreaming in a foreign language important to you? Why?
Give them five minutes for this written stage and then invite them to pair off and exchange their thoughts.

TASK 17—THE MOAT AND THE JUG

You want to get across to a square tower.

The tower has a square moat, full of deep water.

The moat is ten metres across.

You have two metal ladders, both eight metres long.

You must get across to the tower <u>without getting wet</u>—how can you do this?

A group of you have bought a barrel of beer.

One person in the group, John, is determined to drink exactly one litre of beer, neither more nor less.

You look around the house to find something to measure with—all you can find is a three litre jug.

Then someone else finds a five litre jug.

How are you going to give John his one litre of beer?

Solution
As the moat is a square one, place one ladder across one corner and then the second ladder should reach from the edge of the first ladder across to the tower.

Solution
Draw three litres from the barrel in the three litre jug and then pour it into the five litre one. Draw another three litres in the three litre jug and pour what you can of it into the five litre jug. What is left in the three litre jug will be one litre.

4.4 QUESTION AND ANSWER

TASK 18—THE PHONE BOX

The mystery story—to be given out to four people in the questioning group. See introduction.

The phone box was made mainly of glass.

There was a man inside.

The receiver was hanging down off the hook.

Outside there was a black bag.

Possible answers—to be shared out among the other half of the class.

The man was dead.

There was blood everywhere in the phone kiosk.

He did not die because of something the other person said.

He was not killed by another person.

He did not *want* to kill himself.

In fact, he *did* kill himself.

He was not crazy.

He was not ill.

He was probably not ringing his wife.

He was not ringing a doctor.

He was ringing a friend.

The contents of the black bag is very important.

There was no money in the bag.

There were no jewels in the bag.

He had his arms out through the glass of the phone booth.

There was an animal in the bag.

The animal was not a mammal.

The animal was a reptile.

It was a fish.

The fish was a very large one.

He put his arms through the glass of the phone box.

He cut his wrists on the glass of the kiosk.

He was an excitable sort of person.

He gesticulated a lot.

He liked to use his arms when he talked.

He didn't ring the police.

He wanted to tell his friend something.

He wanted to tell his friend about the enormous fish.

The man had caught the fish.

The animal was dead.

The fish had been alive before.

He was a fisherman.

His friend was a fisherman, too.

As he explained how enormous the fish was he flung his arms out wide to show its size.

The glass was broken.

The man had not been shot.

Nobody wanted to kill the man.

The black bag belonged to the man in the kiosk.

There is a strong link between the black bag and the man's death.

The bag was too big to bring into the booth.

Solution

The man was a fisherman and he had just caught the most enormous fish he'd ever seen. He rushed to the nearest phone box to tell his friend about it. In so doing, he mimed the size of the fish, broke the glass in the side of the phone booth, slashed his wrists and bled to death.

TASK 19—THE END

The mystery story—to be given out to four people in the questioning group. See introduction.

Something dreadful happened.

A man was passing a window.

As he passed it, he heard a sound.

On hearing the sound he felt terrible regret.

Possible answers—to be shared out among the other half of the class.

He heard a kind of bell.

He didn't hear music.

He didn't hear a radio.

He heard a man-made sound.

The sound wasn't of someone being killed.

In the man's mind, the sound *was* connected to the dreadful thing that had happened.

The sound itself wasn't happy or unhappy.

There was someone else involved with the noise, besides the man.

The sound was of a phone ringing.

The dreadful thing involves death.

The man lived through the dreadful thing happening.

The dreadful thing involved many more people than him.

The dreadful thing was a terrible war.

The dreadful thing was the Third World War.

The man thought he was the last person left on earth.

He thought everybody else had been destroyed in the exchange of nuclear bombs.

The sound related to the man's regret.

He wasn't in his room.

He wasn't walking along the street.

He wasn't inside a building at all.

He was outside.

He was falling.

The phone wasn't in his room.

The phone wasn't in a public call box.

The phone was in a room.

He was falling past the window of the room where the phone was.

He had jumped from the top of the skyscraper.

He wanted to commit suicide.

He wasn't crazy at all.

He wasn't a specially important person.

A machine made the sound.

The man didn't touch the machine.

The man couldn't answer the phone.

The dreadful thing wasn't a coup d'état.

He didn't feel regret because his wife had left him.

He wasn't hoping that someone special would ring him.

He wasn't passing the window horizontally.

He wasn't running past the window.

He was passing the window vertically.

He didn't know who was ringing up.

He wasn't going through the window.

The dreadful thing was not his death.

The dreadful thing was not a natural event.

The man was not pushed off the top of the building.

The man was not forced to jump by someone else.

He deeply regretted not being able to answer the phone.

When he heard the phone ringing, he realised he was *not* the last person left on earth.

When he jumped, he thought he was the last person on earth.

Solution
The Third World War broke out with a terrible exchange of nuclear warheads. The man thought he was the last person left in the world and decided to kill himself by jumping off the top of a skyscraper. Halfway down he heard a phone ringing. Realising he wasn't the sole survivor, he felt terrible regret at committing suicide.